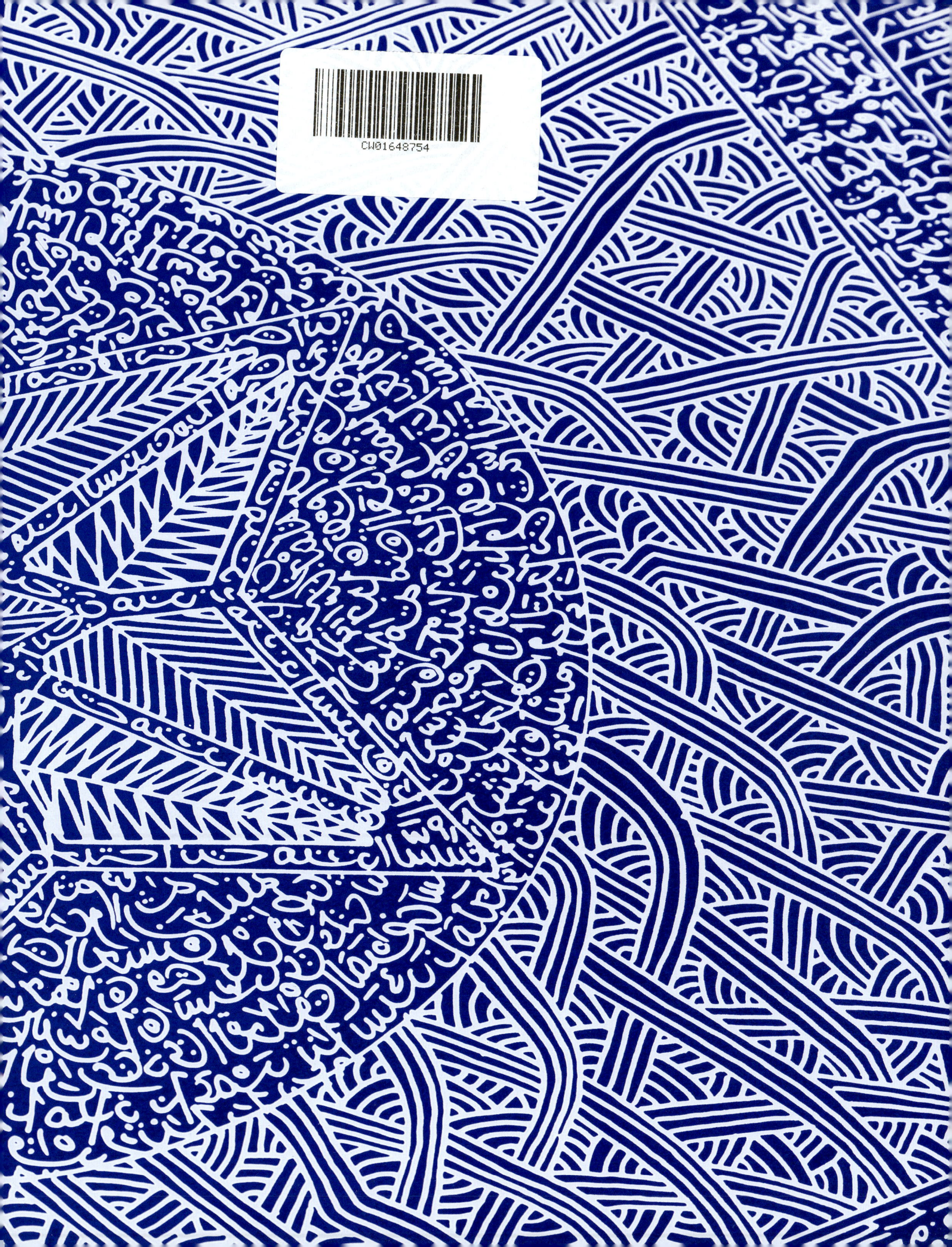

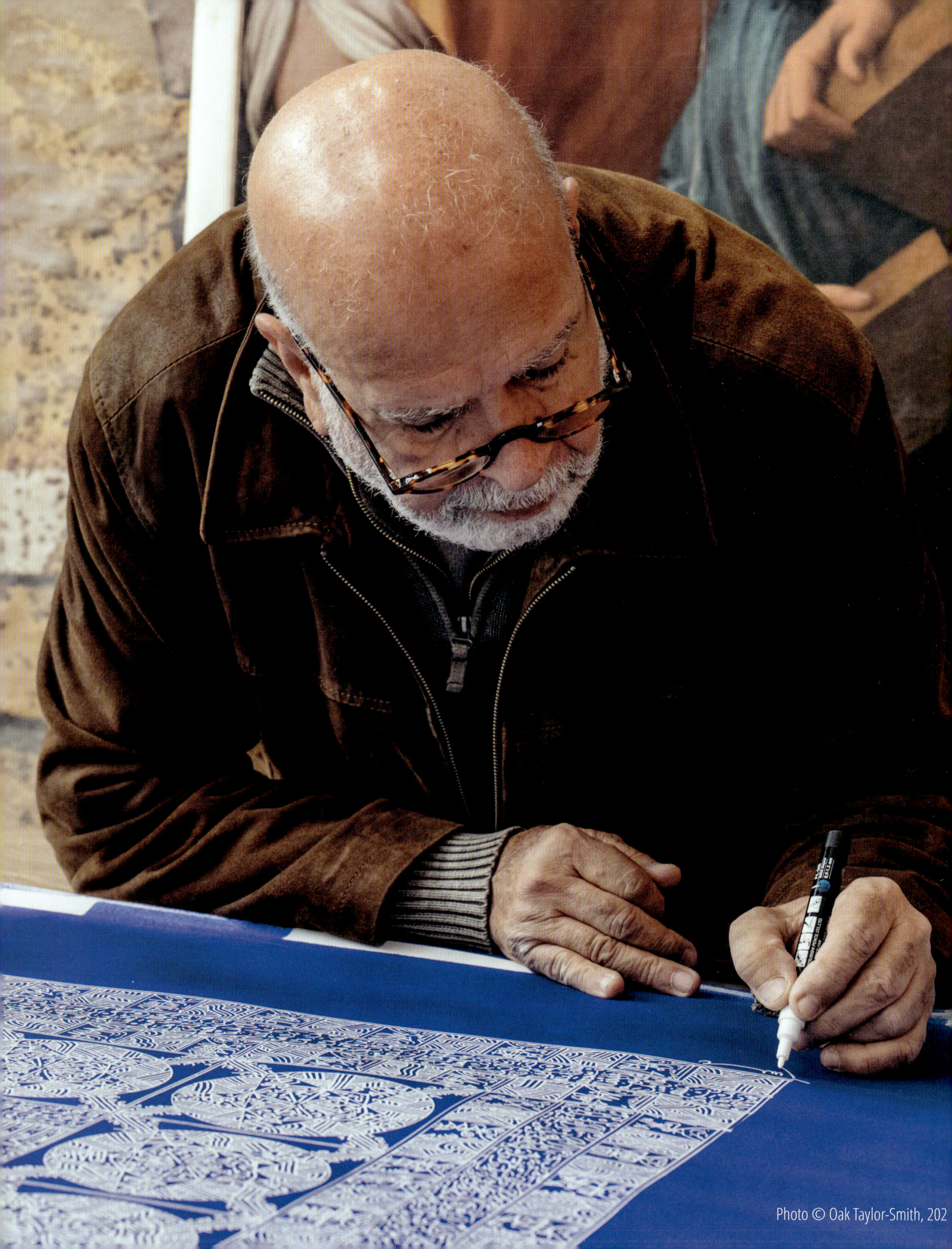
Photo © Oak Taylor-Smith, 202

RACHID KORAÏCHI

In a career spanning over five decades, the Algerian-born artist, Rachid Koraïchi, has created an impressive number of art-works in an astonishing variety of forms: paintings, prints, ceramics, metalwork sculptures, stone-carvings, tapestries, books and printed, or embroidered, linen, cotton and silken textiles. Despite this astonishing diversity of media, Koraïchi's art reflects a unified aesthetic that proposes a broad-minded humanistic system of thought and practice founded upon inherited Sufi wisdom and values.

What is perhaps most remarkable about Koraïchi's creativity is its panoramic sweep, effortlessly shifting from the minute details of his idiosyncratically scripted 'alphabet of signs' to the grand scale of his large installations. At the heart of this extraordinary *corpus* is the irrepressible energy of an artist for whom the finished installation simply marks the completion of a long process of collaborative exchange between many people from different places and traditions. Owing to this multi-modal manner of working, Koraïchi's major installations (*Letters of Clay, Path of Roses, The Invisible Masters, The Prayer of the Absent Ones*, etc.) have each taken many years to reach completion. From that point onwards, Koraïchi's artworks embark upon their own wandering journeys, independently travelling to museums and galleries around the world as the artist's designated representatives.

Informing these collaborative efforts is Koraïchi's understanding of how the Maghrebi and Middle Eastern cultures contribute at least as much to the shared history of the Mediterranean basin as those northern countries commonly seen as the cradle of 'European civilisation.' Koraïchi's more comprehensive culturo-historical perspective reveals how this narrower notion belies the long history of trade, cohabitation, reciprocal influence and vital exchange between these neighbouring spheres of influence over the centuries. Recognising that ignorance provides fertile ground for intolerance, Koraïchi's art proposes alternative perspectives, emphasising how the three major monotheistic 'religions of the book' – Judaism, Christianity and Islam – sharing common regional roots, have always co-existed by opposing violence and promoting tolerance. Few contemporary artists consistently create work whose *raison d'être* exemplifies and embraces a progressive, cultural and social agenda that actively confronts the divisions currently destabilising the world we inhabit together.

This catalogue accompanies *Celestial Blue*, Rachid Koraïchi's sixth solo exhibition at October Gallery. Marking his 77th birthday, in early 2024, the catalogue explores, in his own words, 7 significant themes that tie his multifaceted works into a complex whole. In retracing just a sample of the significant exhibitions that adorn his extraordinary career, it celebrates the life and work of this unique artist and activist.

CELESTIAL BLUE

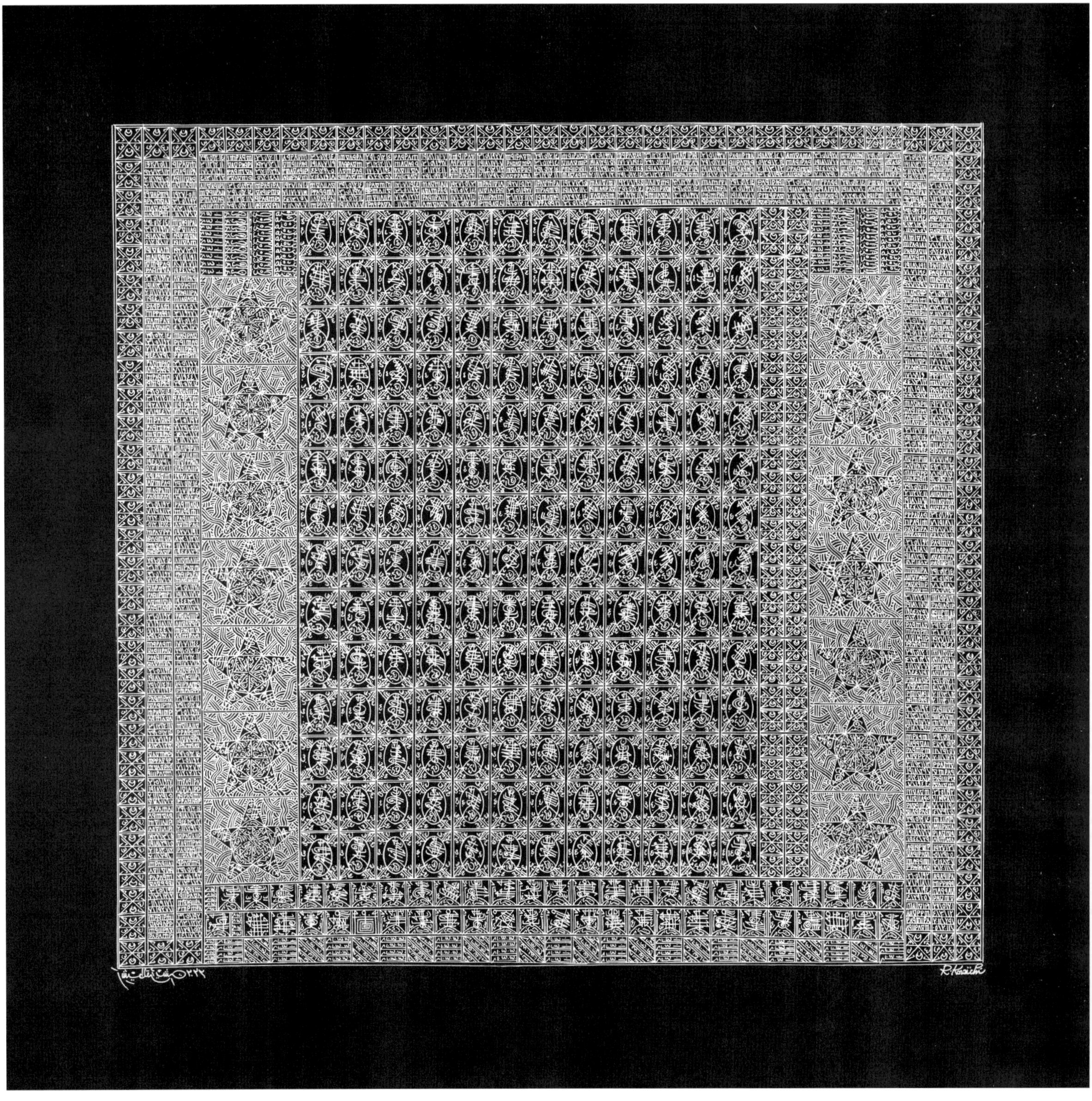

Les ailes bleues des Anges (1) (The Blue of Angels' Wings), 2022.
Acrylic on canvas, 140 x 140 cm.

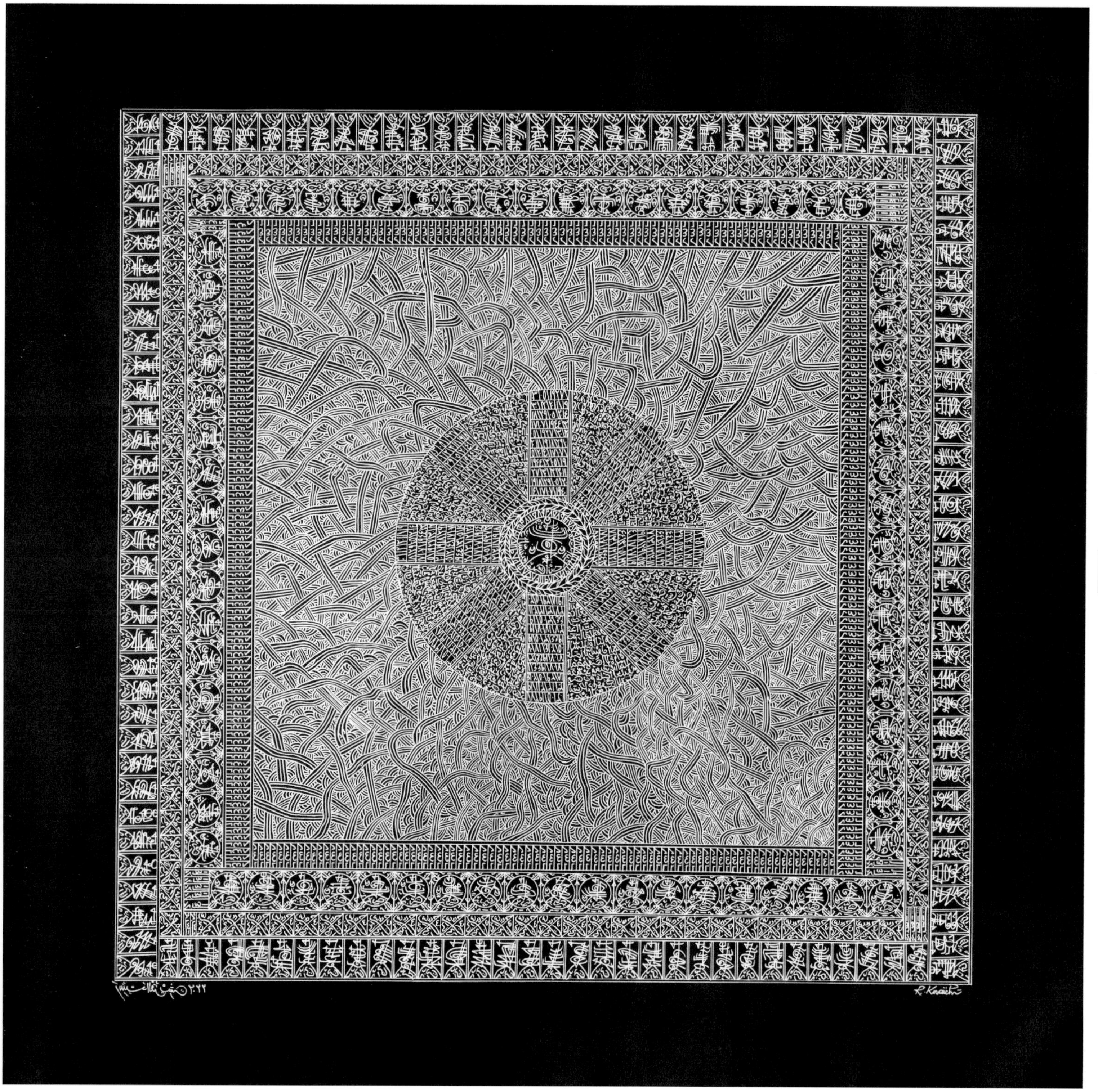

Les ailes bleues des Anges (2) (The Blue of Angels' Wings), 2022.
Acrylic on canvas, 140 x 140 cm.

ANCESTORS

I was born in Ain Beïda, a small town in central Algeria situated between the Mediterranean coast and the Sahara desert to the south. The walls of the house where I was born were covered in writing: Qur'anic texts interwoven with arabesques and geometric figures of plants and animals. Being born into a Sufi community, the written word was everywhere, with scripts penned on parchment, traced on walls or sculpted in alabaster. My infant eyes gazed out upon a world of writing, that I quickly realised, stretched far back in time.

I am entirely influenced by my ancestry; a Sufi family dating from the 7th century, where diversity and freedom of expression were tolerated.

My artistic practice has always drawn on the rich traditions of Sufi mysticism that descended through my ancestral line and within which I grew up. The Quraishi, to which the Prophet Muhammad himself belonged, were an important tribe of scribes based in Mecca. With the expansion of Islam, they radiated out from Mecca reaching all corners of the known world. My direct ancestor, Okba Ibn Amer al-Koraïchi, one of the Prophet's companions, arrived in Algeria in the 7th century, bringing the new religion of Islam and introducing Sufism. Okba led the vanguard of adventurers who travelled further inland, encountering a completely sterile zone – the Great Sahara – where together with their *savoir faire* their faith was also tested. To survive and carry life into that barren zone these courageous men and women needed both dogged persistence and a subtle understanding of the inner nature of things. Failing to recognise the debt we owe our forebears risks losing the knowledge they struggled to accumulate, and ensured they transmitted to us in order that we too can survive.

I think there are several kinds of ancestors: for example those of family, directly linked by blood or those with whom one shares a particular region or environment. While attending the Beaux Arts School in Algiers, I travelled for many days across the unforgiving Sahara, to visit the prehistoric dwellings of the Tassili n'Ajjer plateau. I was amazed by the array of ancient rock paintings – images of moving bison, elephants and immense giraffes – stretching across the inner walls of caves. I had the uncanny realisation that I was gazing at signs left behind by my own ancestors. These original artists were surely painting and sculpting both for the pleasure of the experience and to communicate things of importance amongst themselves. Thousands of years later, their friezes still remain eloquently expressive, and I revelled in being able to drink in directly the messages they had left us, using only reeds for paintbrushes and crushed silica stones as dyes. These ancestral artists still offer important insights into the artist's role today.

By consciously weaving these twin ancestral transmissions together – the profound *signatures* of these cave-dwelling ancestors and the mystical insights of my Sufi forebears – I endeavour to reinvigorate the ancient signs and mysterious scripts that retrace the buried tales of our shared inheritance.

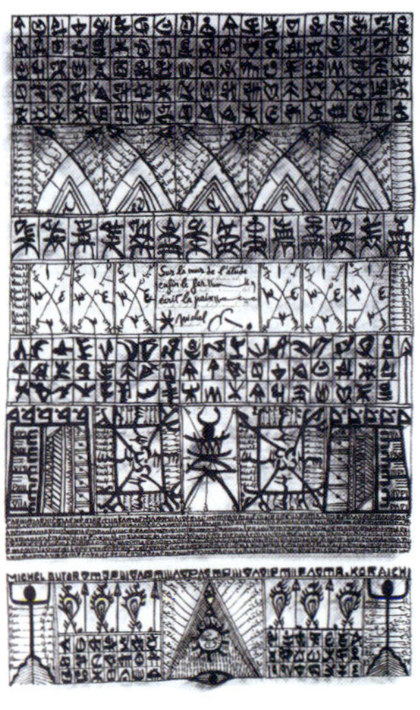

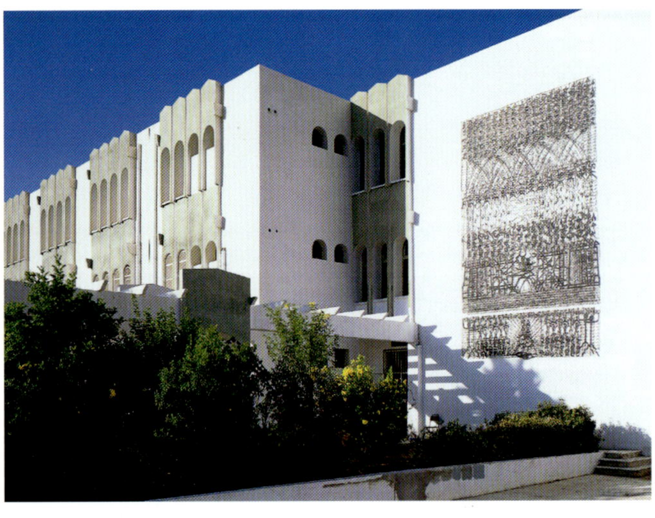

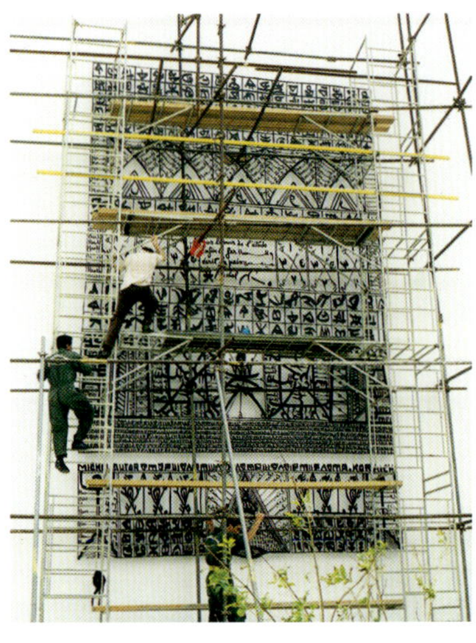

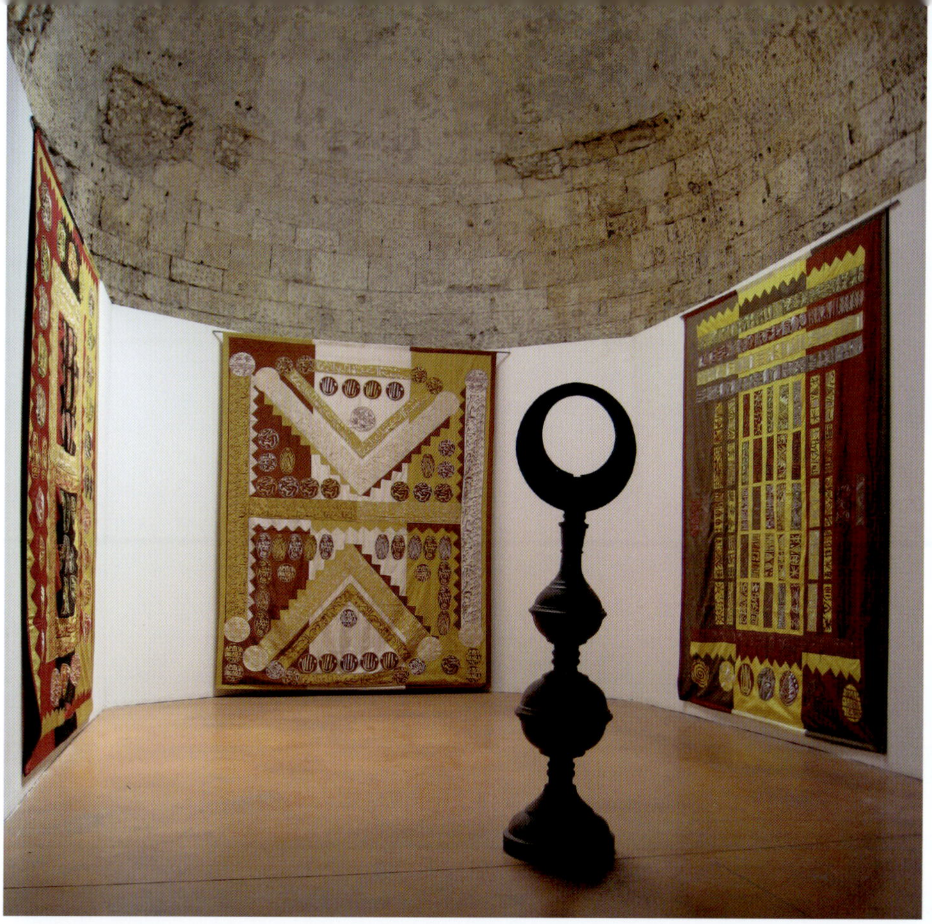

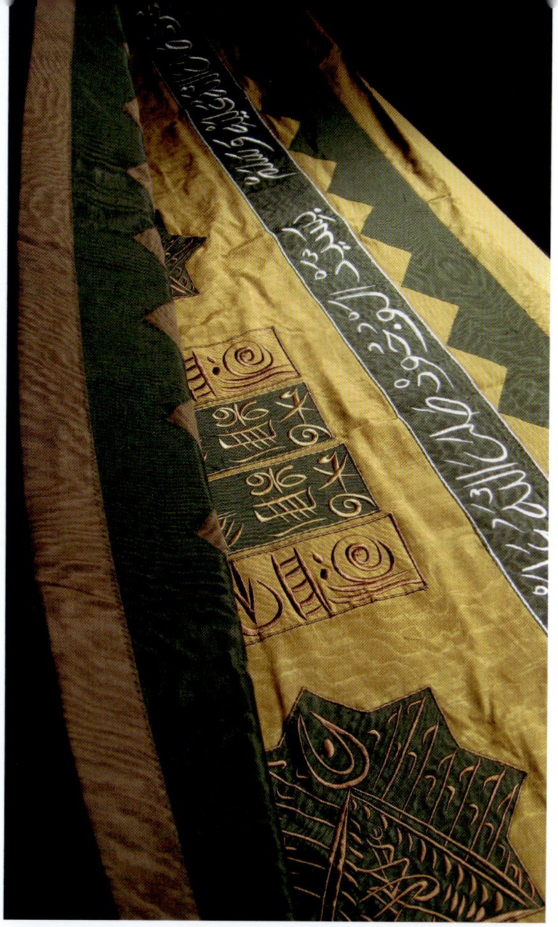

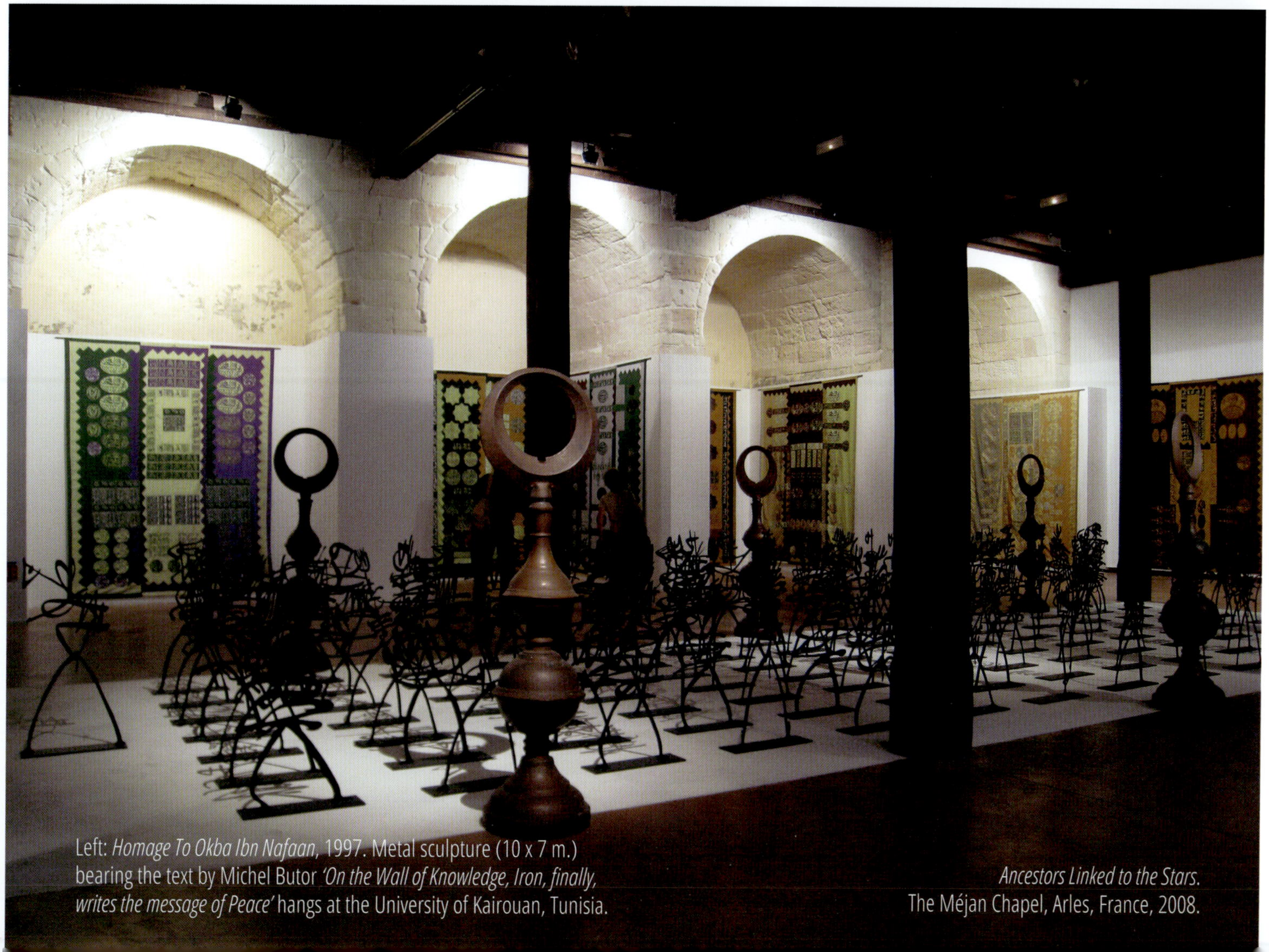

Left: *Homage To Okba Ibn Nafaan,* 1997. Metal sculpture (10 x 7 m.) bearing the text by Michel Butor *'On the Wall of Knowledge, Iron, finally, writes the message of Peace'* hangs at the University of Kairouan, Tunisia.

Ancestors Linked to the Stars.
The Méjan Chapel, Arles, France, 2008.

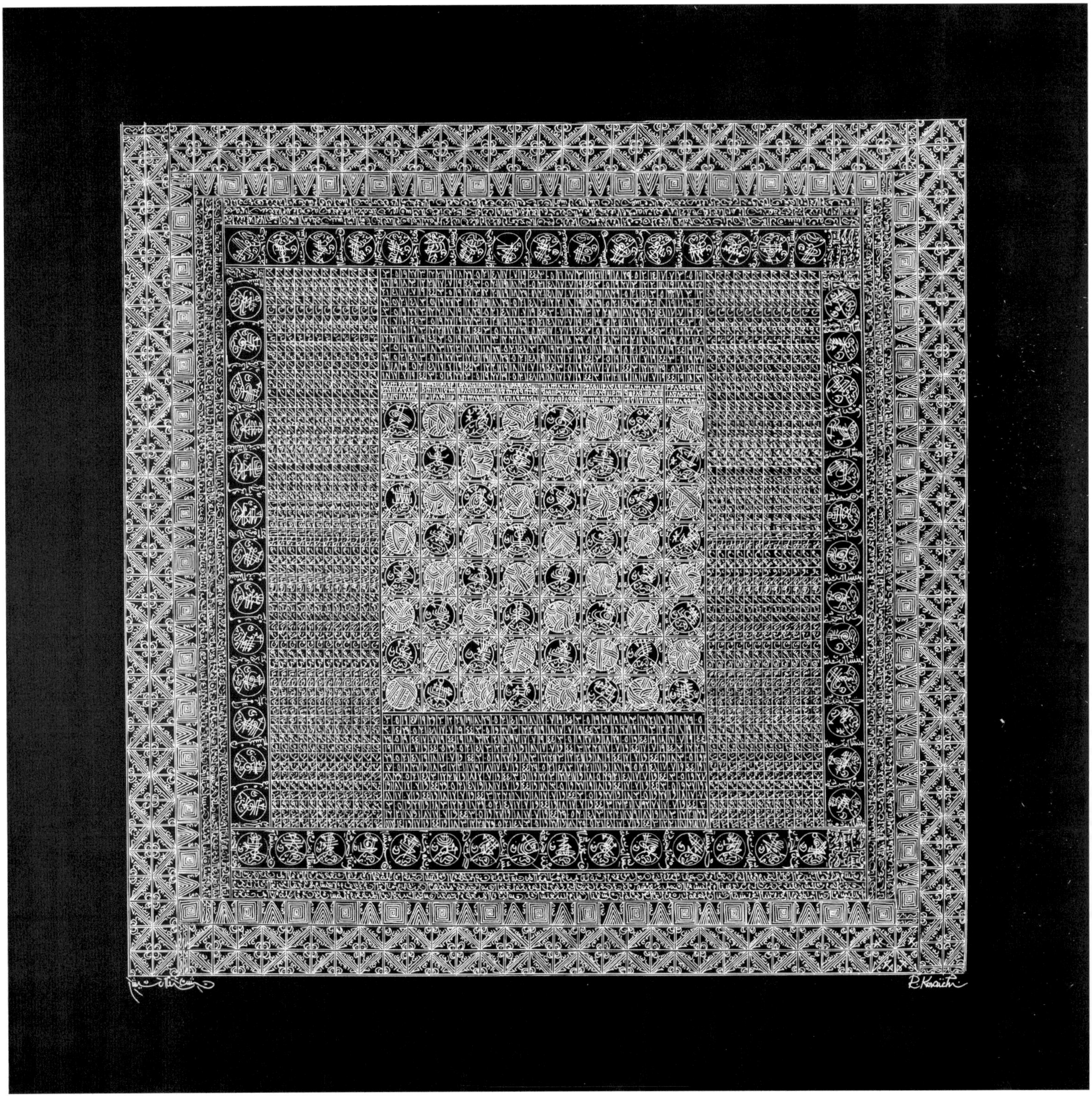

Les ailes bleues des Anges (3) (The Blue of Angels' Wings), 2022.
Acrylic on canvas, 140 x 140 cm.

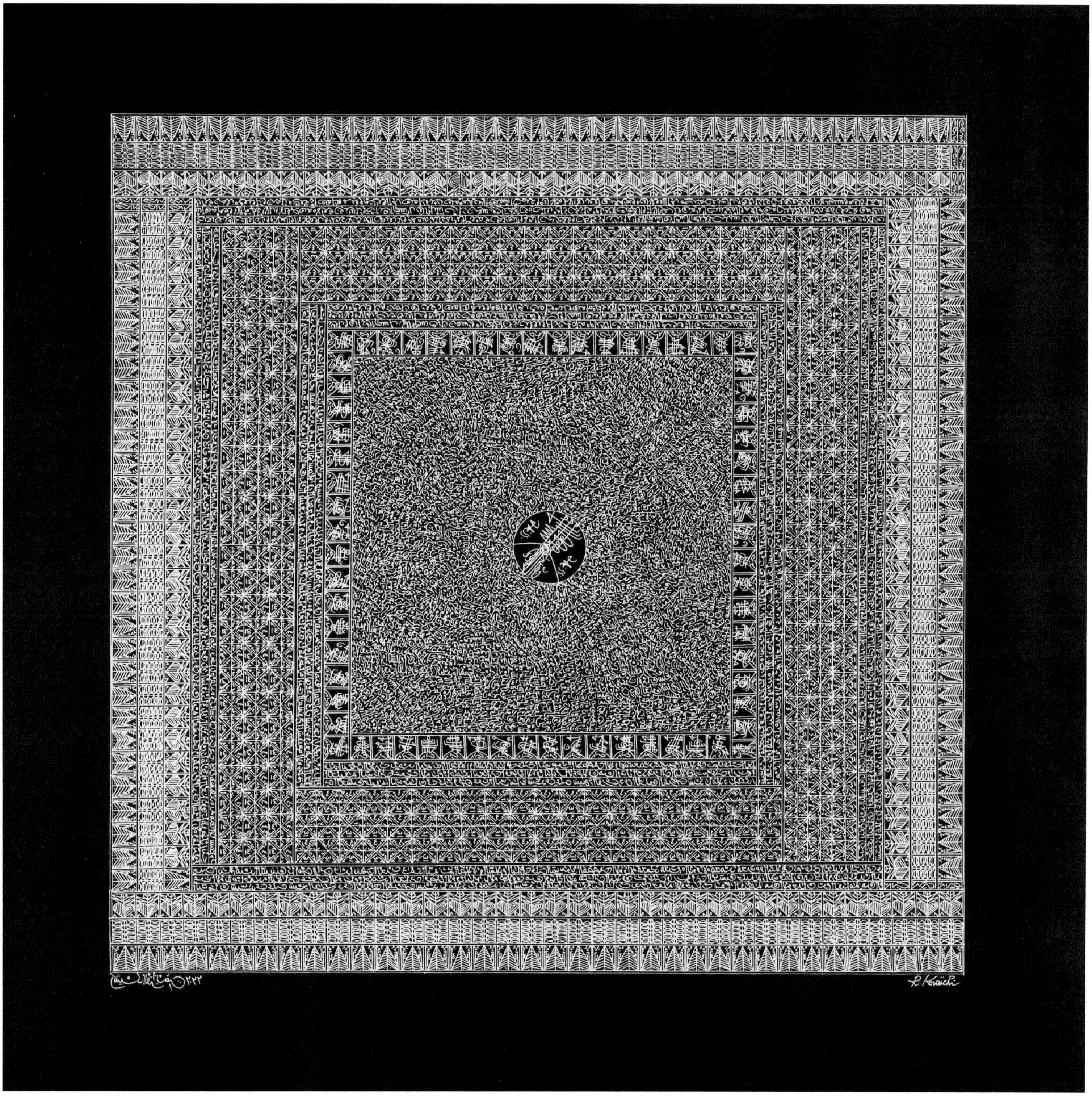

Les ailes bleues des Anges (4) (The Blue of Angels' Wings), 2022.
Acrylic on canvas, 140 x 140 cm.

COLLABORATION

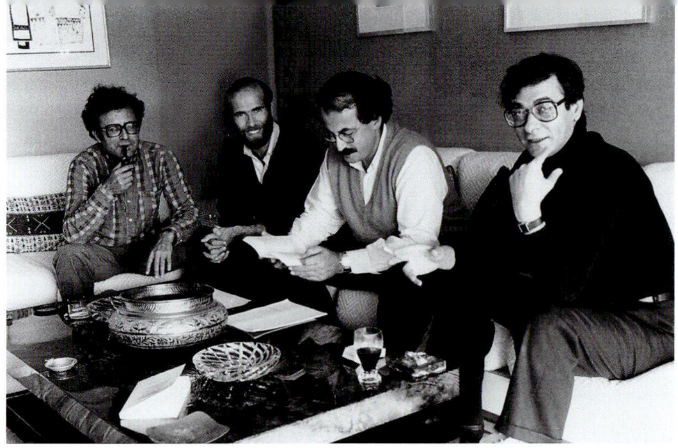

I have always felt the necessity of collaborating with other creative types – be they poets, musicians, writers, dancers or theatre people – with whom, over time, I've enjoyed working to weave together multi-media projects. To name just a few of the inspirational authors and poets with whom I've been privileged to work: Michel Butor, Nancy Huston, Mahmoud Darwish, John Berger, Hassan Massoudy, Mohamed Dib, René Char… the list goes on!

Although my formation as an artist is based on classical training at the leading Fine Arts schools of the west, my sources of influence extend much further back again, to include those early "makers" who created the magnificent friezes adorning the walls of the caves at Tassili, Lascaux, Drakensburg, and so on. These "ancestors" produced their astonishing works independently of other groups and their works co-existed in complete artistic equality. They were certainly produced by many hands, with supplementary layers added over time. Today's art market is based on a hierarchy of individual artists, and fluctuating market forces dictate what is considered valuable and *à la mode*. Unsurprisingly, western artists predominate, while Indigenous peoples and those of the African and Islamic worlds are often considered subaltern derivatives, barely attaining to the level of "Art."

My work aims to unite peoples and cultures by their shared inheritance, in spite of the tendencies for national boundaries and culturally-conditioned patterns of thought to separate them.

My own practice involves systematic collaboration with craftsmen of ancient and uninterrupted Islamic traditions, including weavers, dyers, metal-workers and potters from Egypt, Iraq, Syria, Morocco, Tunisia, and beyond. Their hand-made works provide vital bridges connecting contemporary creativity and a disappearing body of knowledge that dates back many centuries. Their skills flourished during ages when the great Sufi masters, Ibn 'Arabi, Rumi and Attar were alive. My work aims to sustain and celebrate these historical traditions of practice and thought by employing various strategies that are guided by the ethos and numerology of Sufism. My hope is to combine the formal and esoteric qualities of practices in order to disseminate the sublime beauties of the Islamic tradition.

Artists and artisans of the Islamic world are linked together in a long tradition of non-figuration, passed down from master to student over time. These fabricators developed a graphic intelligence that, whilst remaining within an abstract frame, was capable of conveying weighty ideas of great subtlety and depth. This maturing instinct pushed formal abstraction into novel areas at the highest of intellectual levels. Only in the early 20th century did such great western artists as Braque, Klee, Picasso and Matisse, trained within the western paradigm of figurative representation, begin to develop another kind of abstraction.

Since I want to work only with artists of the highest quality, I am aware of contemporary practitioners whose work achieves extraordinary levels of perfection. That is the reason I collaborate so closely with the gifted artists, craftspeople and scientists who gather at Factum Arte in Madrid. They use the most advanced techniques of material science known today to analyse, repair and reproduce the wonders of art bequeathed to us by masters of the ancient world. They truly are contemporary masters, at the forefront of a developing field entirely of their own making.

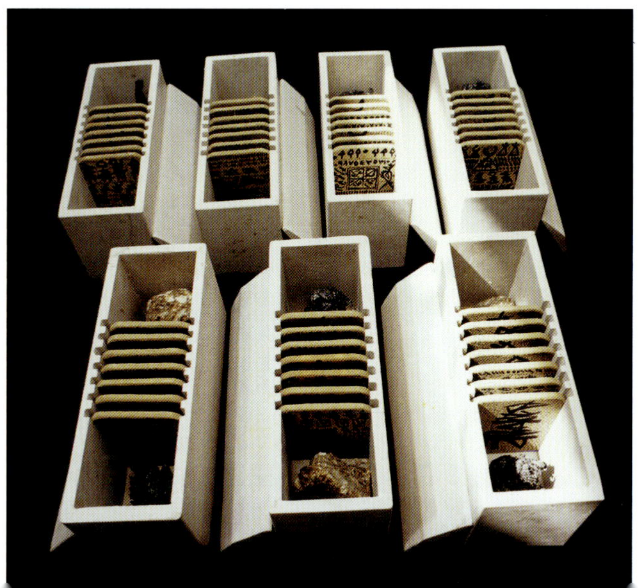

Left: Abdelkebir Khatibi, Rachid Koraïchi, Elias Sanbar and Mahmoud Darwish, 1988.

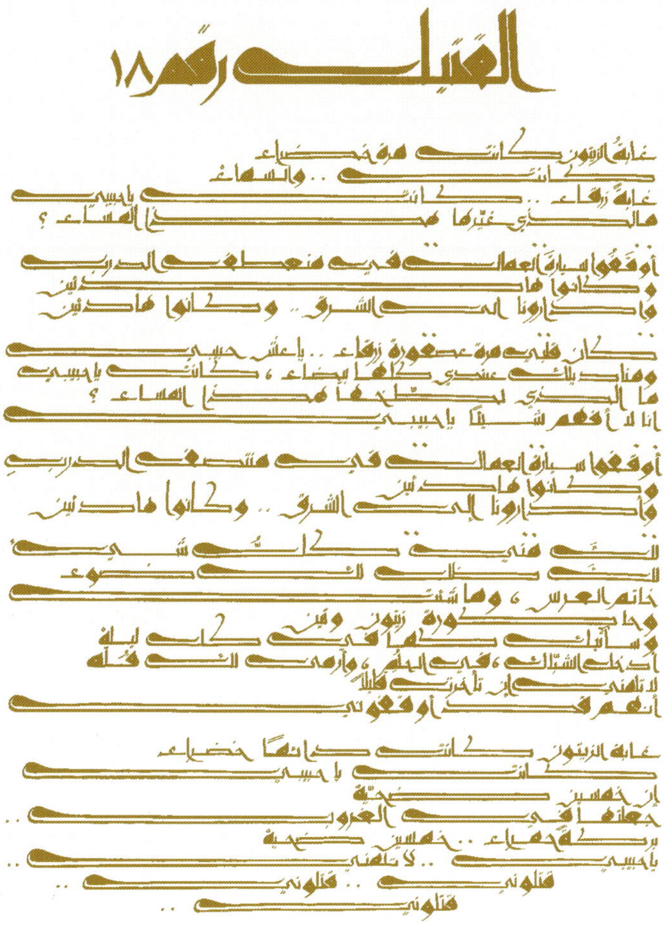

Below: *A Nation In Exile: Engraved Hymns (Une Nation en Exil: Hymnes Gravés)* ,1981.
Text by Mahmoud Darwish, calligraphy by Hassan Massoudy.
Lithographs, 76 x 56 cm.

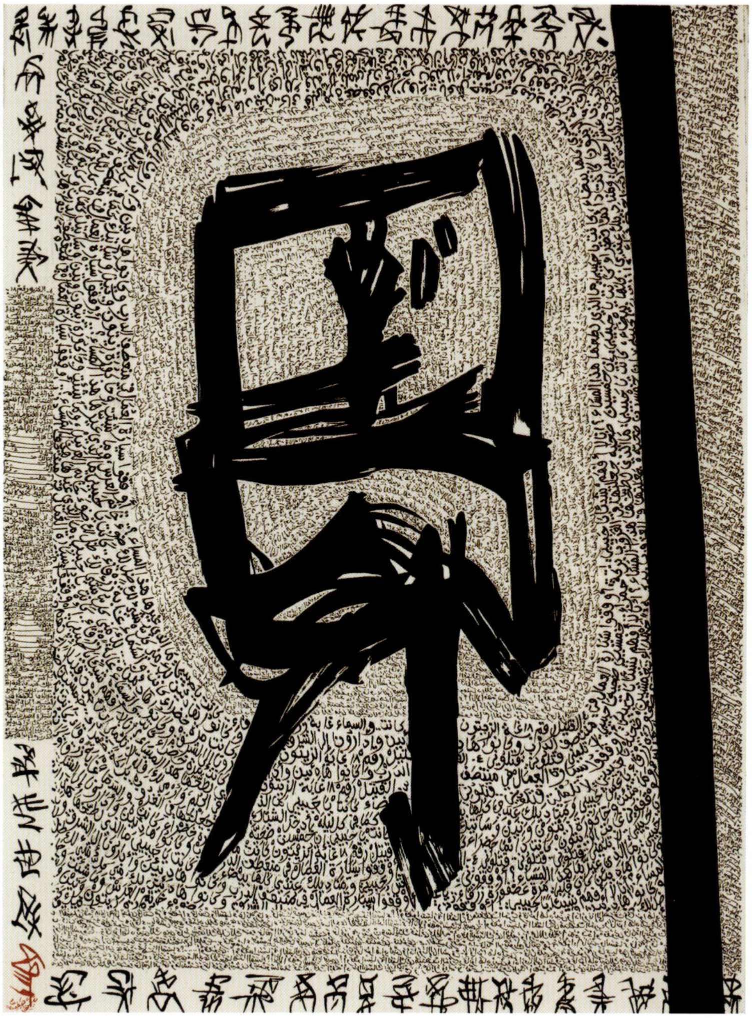

Below: *'Faire Du Chemin Avec……René Char'.*
Group installation, Palais des Papes, Avignon, France, 1990.
Featuring (left to right): *Eternal Couple,* Egypt 3000 AD,
Couple, bronze by Georges Braque,
Saint Agatha of Zurbaran, *For René Char* by Rachid Koraïchi, installed above, *Seven Magic Sculptures* by Rachid Koraïchi.
Bottom left: View inside *Seven Magic Sculpture*s with 7 clay tablets and 7 incense balls in each sarcophagus.

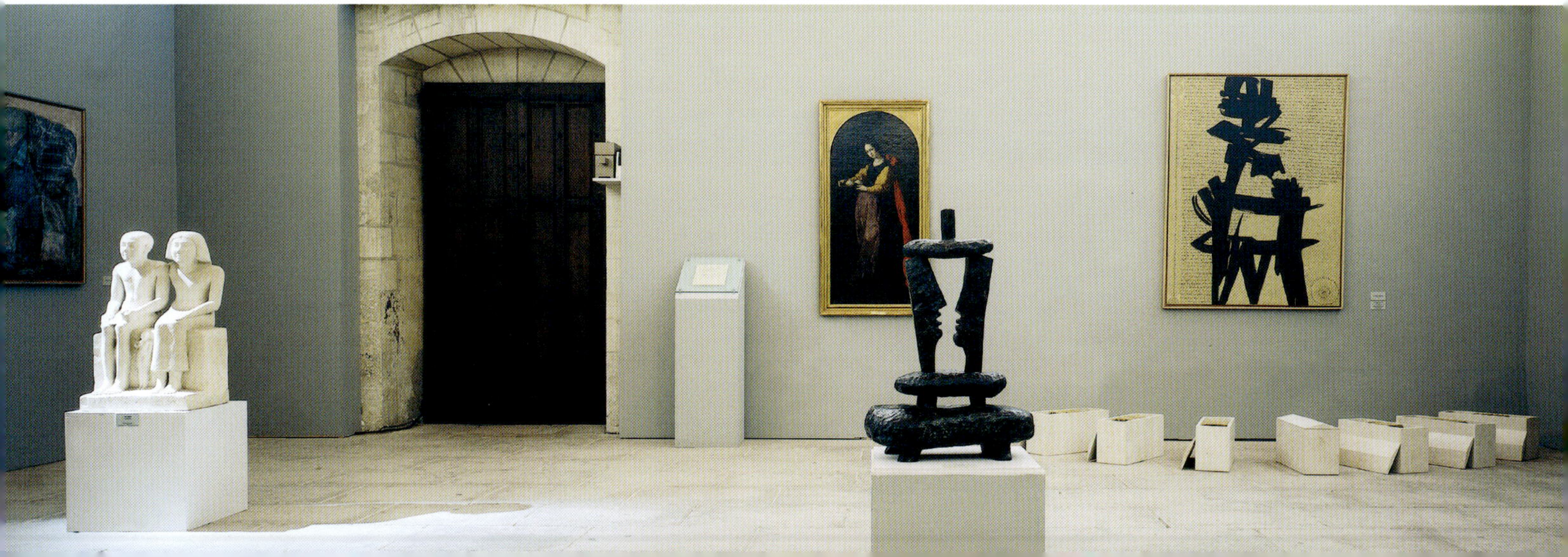

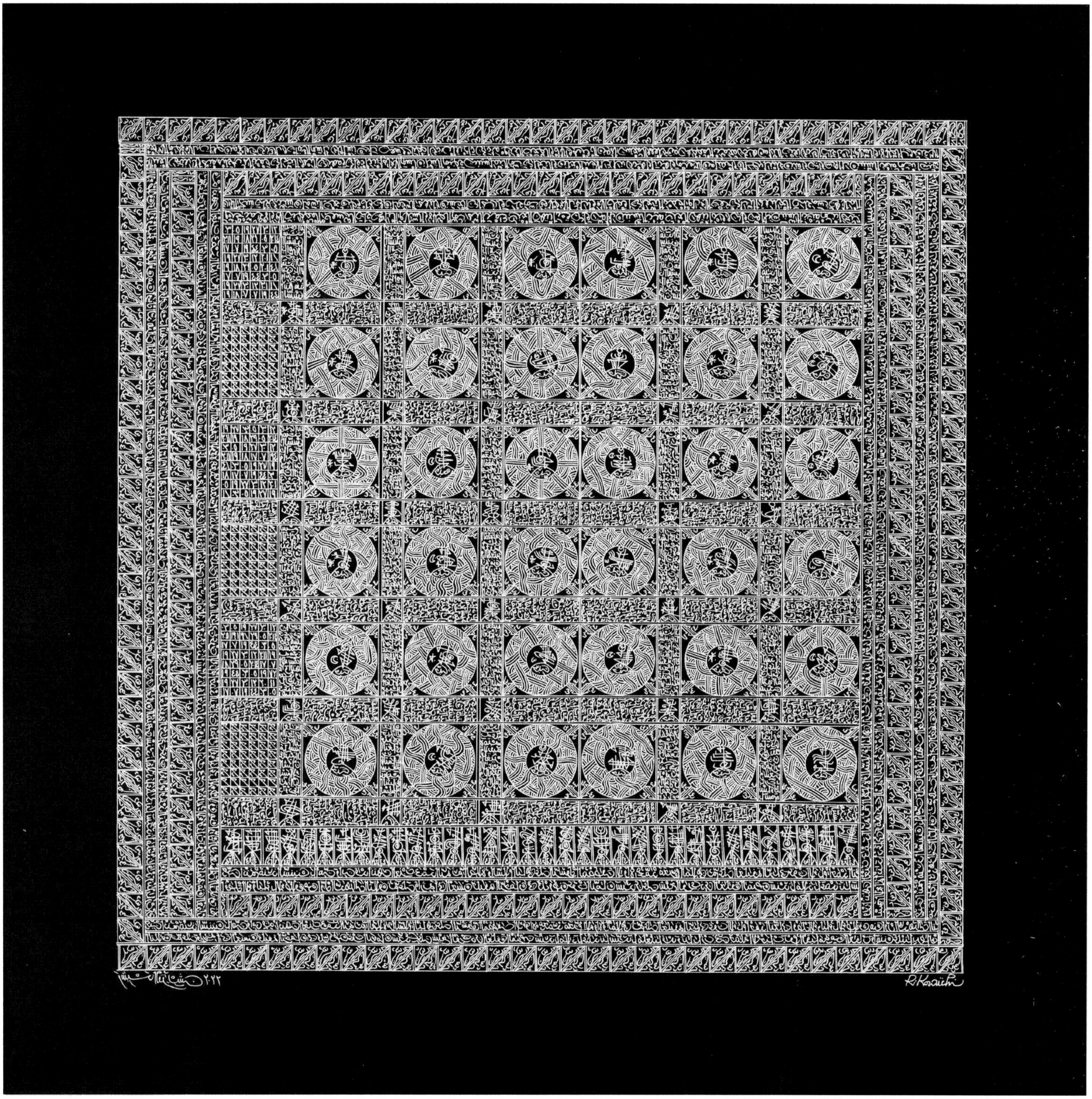

Les ailes bleues des Anges (5) (The Blue of Angels' Wings), 2022.
Acrylic on canvas, 140 x 140 cm.

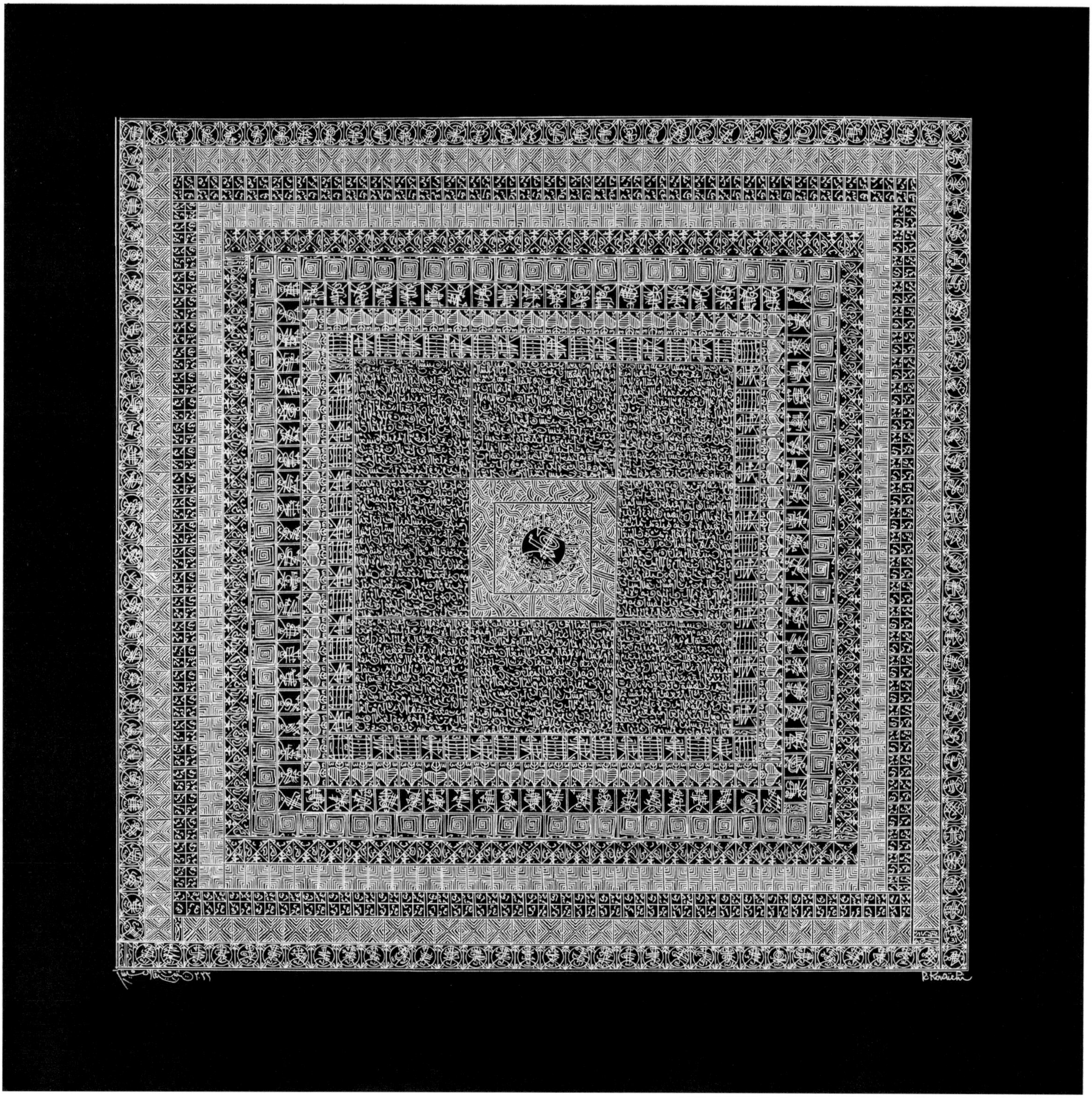

Les ailes bleues des Anges (6) (The Blue of Angels' Wings), 2022.
Acrylic on canvas, 140 x 140 cm.

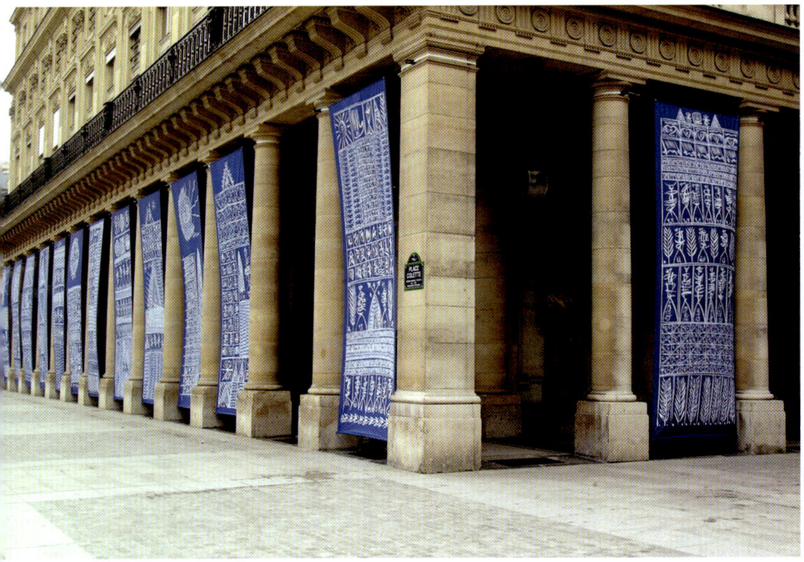

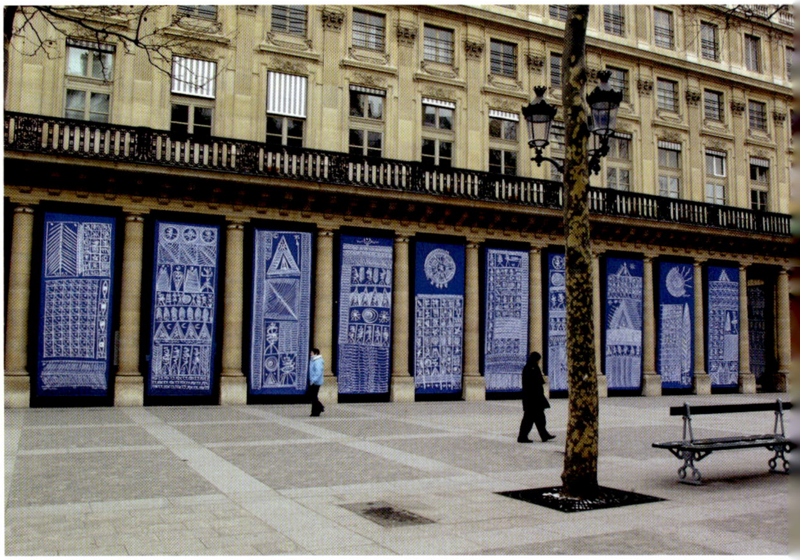

Above: *Fragments of Script (Frangments d'écriture).*
Comédie Français, Paris, France, 2003.

Below: *Ecstatic Flow.*
October Gallery, London, UK, 2011.

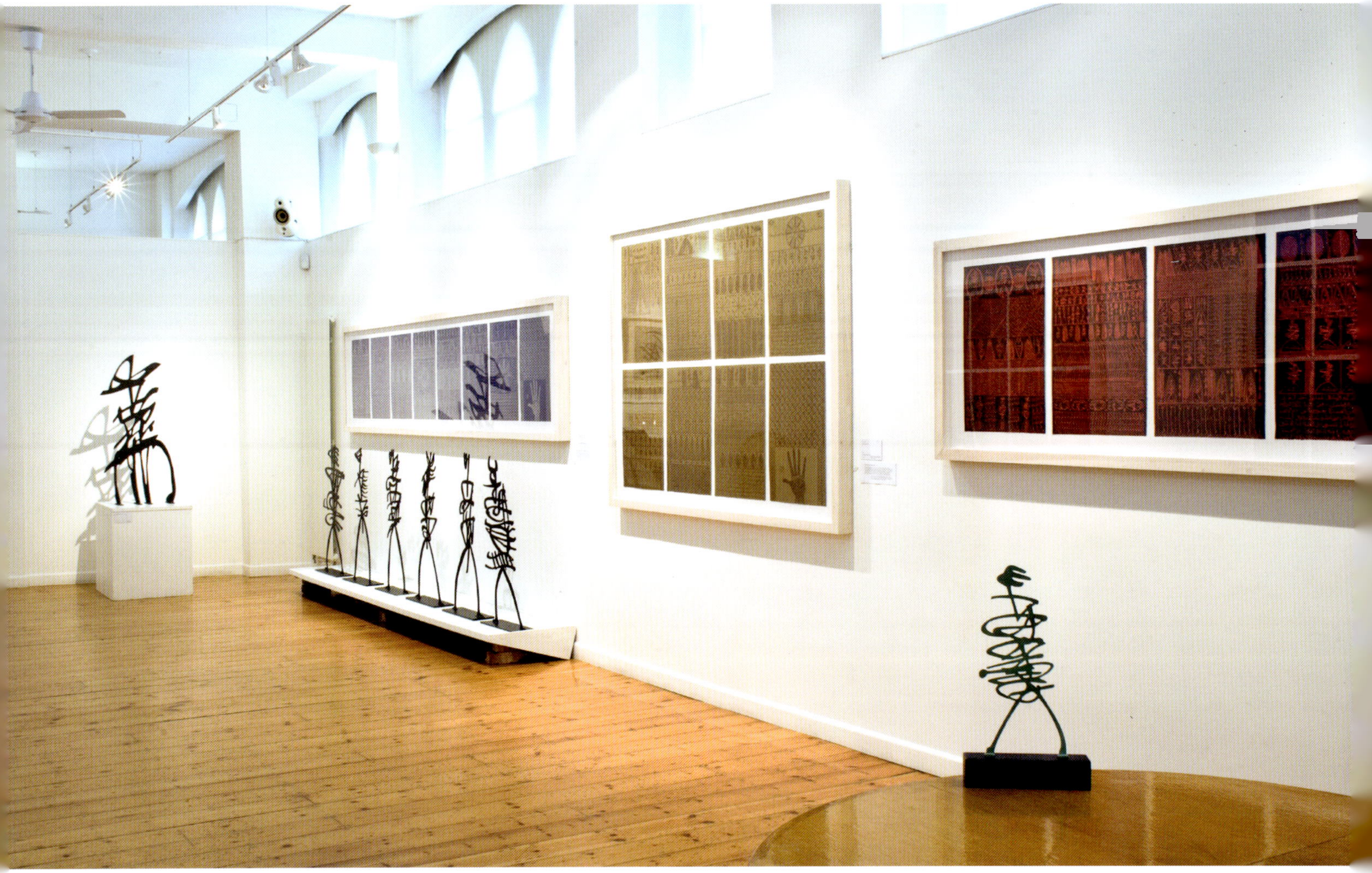

SCRIPTS & NUMBERS

Throughout the entire Muslim world, where the written word is seen as a reflection of the word of God, writing is considered absolutely fundamental. My work is based on this civilisation of the written word, and the associational possibilities of signs, whether in two or three-dimensional forms. But writing and drawing, arising, as it were, from the same breath, are gesturally speaking identical.

To be enamoured with written lines composed of signs and symbols is to be in love with that universal culture which is our human heritage. I've always wanted people to appreciate this universal aspect of my work. By this I mean, to see my work in terms of the symbols, signs and marks which form the common language of mankind, our shared inheritance, and of which many examples remain as rock art existing since the dawn of time. Whether in Lascaux or Tassili such art is easily decipherable by all. We interpret these surviving traces instinctively, the way weavers of carpets read woven forms, or signs traced on pottery reveal secrets about other civilisations. To this pre-existing crucible of signs, I add my own humble offerings, hoping to extend the repertory of universal symbols available to the world.

My work is about the power of gestures, whether they be gestures of language, or again those of mathematical and geometrical forms.

Symbols appropriated from different cultures woven together with remnants of archaic alphabets, interspersed with magic squares, sun and moon signs or spontaneous abstract inventions self-organise into expressive wholes. This associative proto-language points towards a common set of experiences and aspirations shared by all mankind: a notional language of hope that is legible to all and to which every culture can subscribe.

Another abstracted sign language bordering on the universal, which fascinated early Arab scholars, was mathematics. For many years now, my work has been based upon the number seven, an auspicious number charged with numerological significance, and not just for the Sufi orders alone, but for a wide variety of other traditions too. 'Lucky seven' is acknowledged in the Jewish, Christian, Islamic, Buddhist and Taoist traditions. Our ancestors were aware of seven's significance because of the seven celestial beings that governed time and space. The ancients therefore linked the sun, the moon and the five 'wandering' planets to the seven days of the week, Sunday, Mo(o)nday and so on.

This 'magical' prime number is deeply embedded in all my work. In the Sufi tradition, 7 signifies perfection, and it is said that every verse, word and letter of the Qur'an can be interpreted on seven separate levels of significance. In all of my exhibitions and installations, not only the number of pieces displayed, but their dimensions and even the spaces separating them will generally be found to be some multiple of this potent number. Whether this fact rises to the conscious level of perception or not, all of my installations exist in a world that reflects this harmonious logic of perfection projected onto the underlying geometries of the surrounding space.

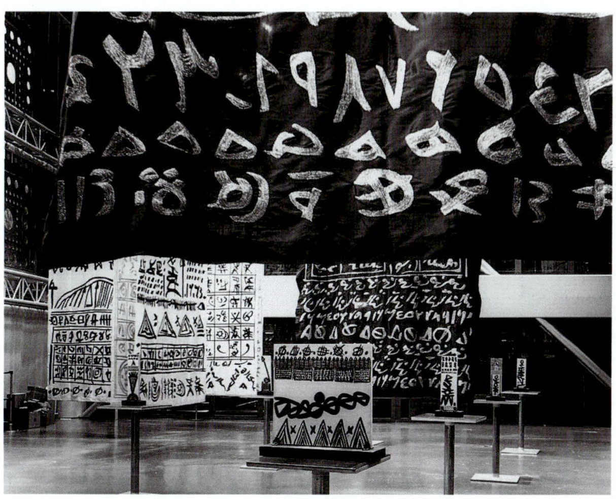

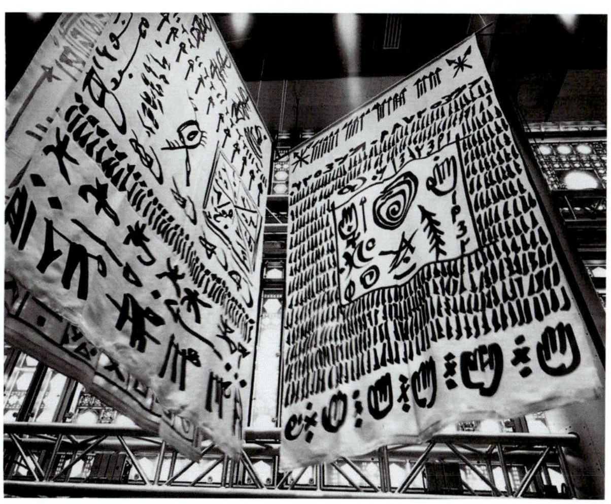

Salomé,
Centre Pompidou,
Paris, 1990.

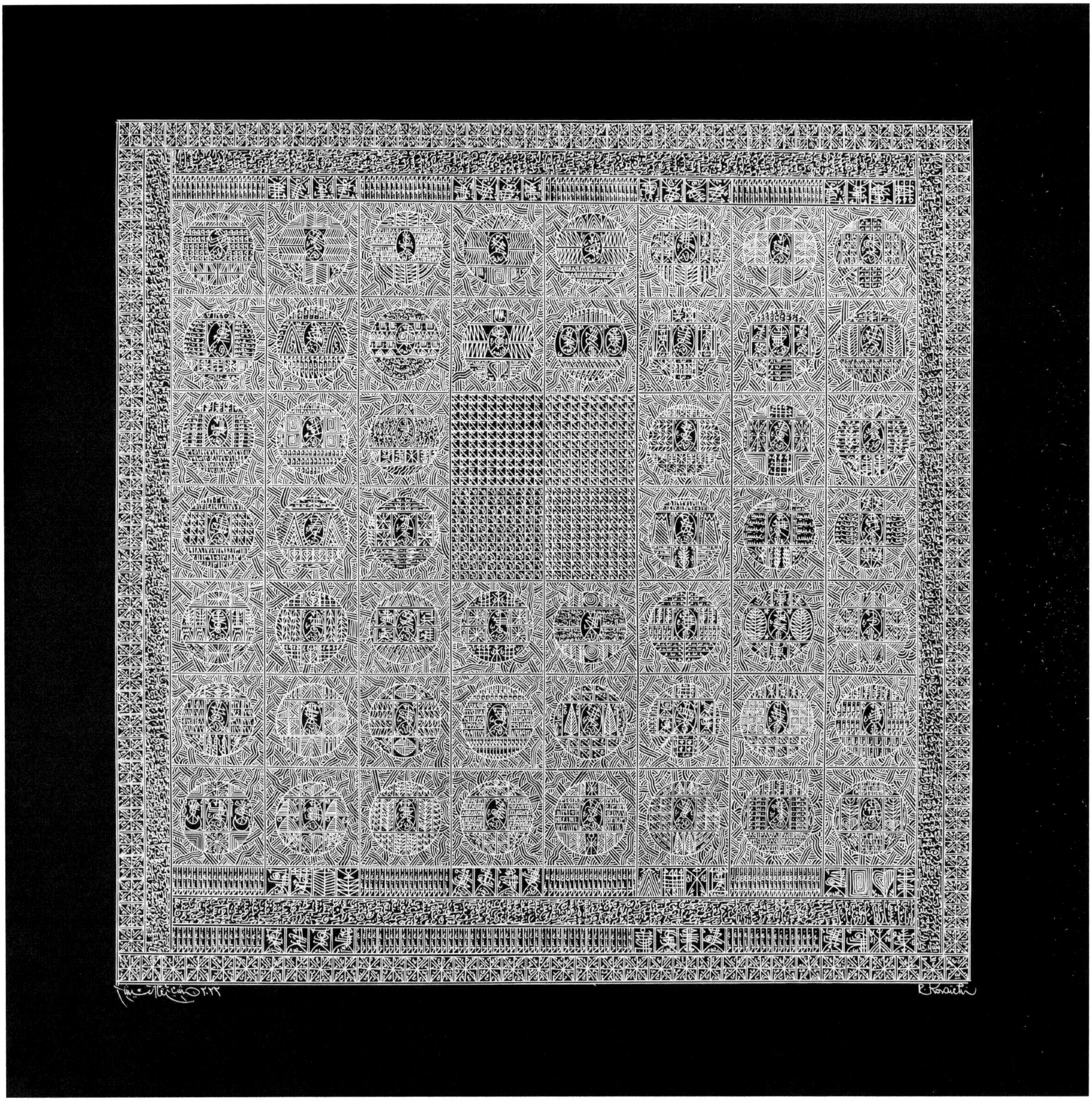

Les ailes bleues des Anges (13) (The Blue of Angels' Wings), 2022.
Acrylic on canvas, 140 x 140 cm.

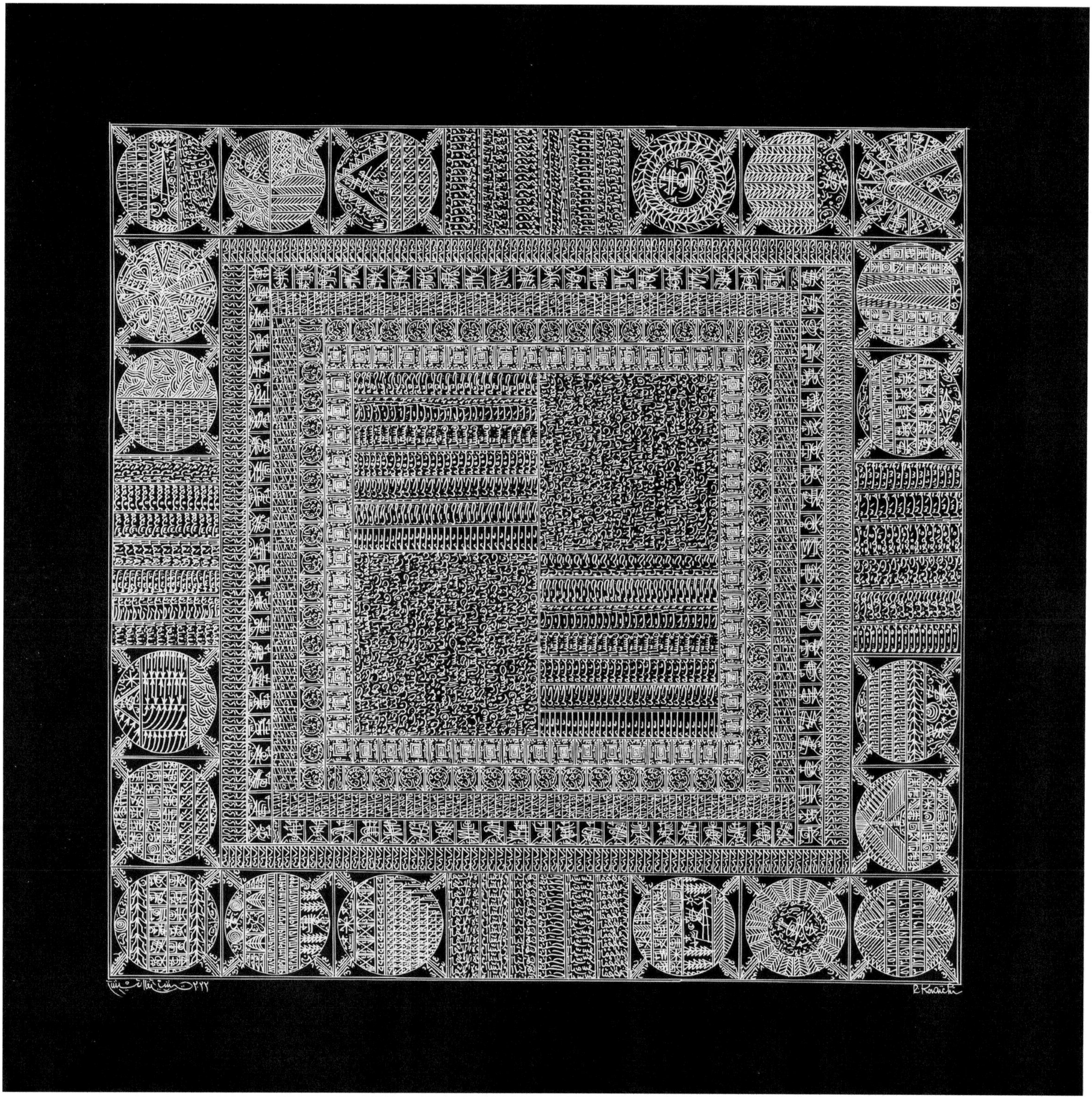

Les ailes bleues des Anges (14) (The Blue of Angels' Wings), 2022.
Acrylic on canvas, 140 x 140 cm.

CELESTIAL BLUE

I'm fascinated by the wandering life and writings of one of the Islamic world's most important mystical thinkers, Muhyi al-Din ibn 'Arabi. Born in Andalucia, Spain, Ibn 'Arabi first travelled across north Africa and the Middle East, before visiting Mecca and eventually settling in Damascus, Syria. An earlier project devoted to him, the *Letters of Clay* series, had to be restarted from scratch after torrential rain destroyed 21 hand-painted jars during a night-firing on the Tunisian island of Djerba. Another major project, *Path of Roses*, imagines Ibn 'Arabi meeting with his contemporary the poet Rumi, and both also figure among the 14 Sufi sages addressed in *The Invisible Masters*.

To Muslims, Ibn 'Arabi is considered at least as significant a mystic and writer as St. Augustine is to Christians. This canvas series, *The Blue of Angels' Wings*, draws inspiration from the 61 love poems (*nasibs*) found in his *Tarjuman al-Ashwaq, The Interpreter of Desire,* published in 1215. Each square canvas presents unique geometrical designs in white script on a blue ground, created as free-hand improvisations reflecting one poem of the set. Rather than being direct translations, however, the canvases respond to the profundity of Ibn 'Arabi's lyrical outpourings, offering a visual correlative in a geometrically structured graphical form. By embroidering each work with corresponding symbols, I try to register each poem's 'atmosphere' and allow the hidden depths of the mystical texts to surface. This provides another way of approaching these exquisite poems that explore the mysteries of love, whether it be love of another person or love for the divine. These complex poems also treat of life and its complementary opposite, death, which arrives as time disappears.

From the outset, I wanted the works to be both large and square. This refers to the Ka'bah in Mecca, which is cubic in shape. The square also has direct links to the earth, as all architectural designs or plots begin with a four-sided figure. For colours I wanted to use a deep blue to embody the depths of infinite space, the celestial realm of the heavens. Blue is also the colour of invisibility. The most appropriate way of making a distinct mark on this heavenly ground must be the purest of whites. For me, blue and white are the colours of life itself. I imagine a tiny white cloud passing across the immense face of a brilliantly blue sky. But that white cloud, made of wisps of tenuous vapour, is at the mercy of the slightest gust of wind, which will dissipate it in an instant. For me this suggests how our transit through life is no more than a brief passage of uncertain chance.

The canvas could have been covered in blue before overpainting in white, but working with coloured pigments can lead to blockages. To enable these scripts to stream forth without resistance, I began by using a fine paintbrush and *encre-de-chine* on white paper. I never make prior sketches or block out any initial design, but begin working directly on the page so that the fluid letters and symbols pour out in a torrent of inspiration that continues until the page is perfectly filled. The magic of transforming the white page into a blue ground and the black ink into its inverse of white is undertaken by the genius of our friends at Factum Arte, who convert the colours of the creation process into the particular colours that I wish to employ. This underlines the mysteries of mutability: white ground into blue, the colour of invisibility; and black script into white words and symbols, expressing the colour of purity.

Most memorable for me was working with the Palestinian poet, Mahmoud Darwish, in Tunis...It was never a question of merely "illustrating" his poems - a sheer impossibility. Instead, I wanted to react aesthetically by capturing the emotional charge from which each poem springs.

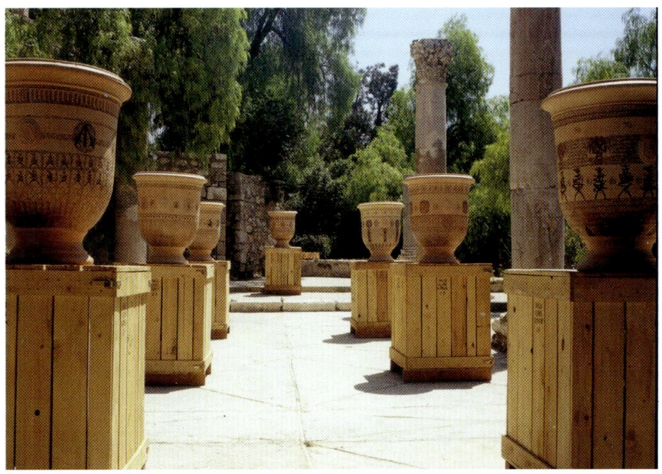

Installation of the *Letters of Clay (Lettres d'argile) Homage to Ibn Arabi*, 1995.
Shoman Foundation, Darat-al-Funun, Amman, Jordan, 1998.
Anduze Vases (Versailles Model), clay, 85 x 75 cm. (Studio of Le Chêne Vert, Anduze).

Opposite page: *Les ailes bleues des Anges* (detail), 2022.
Acrylic on canvas, 150 x 150 cm.

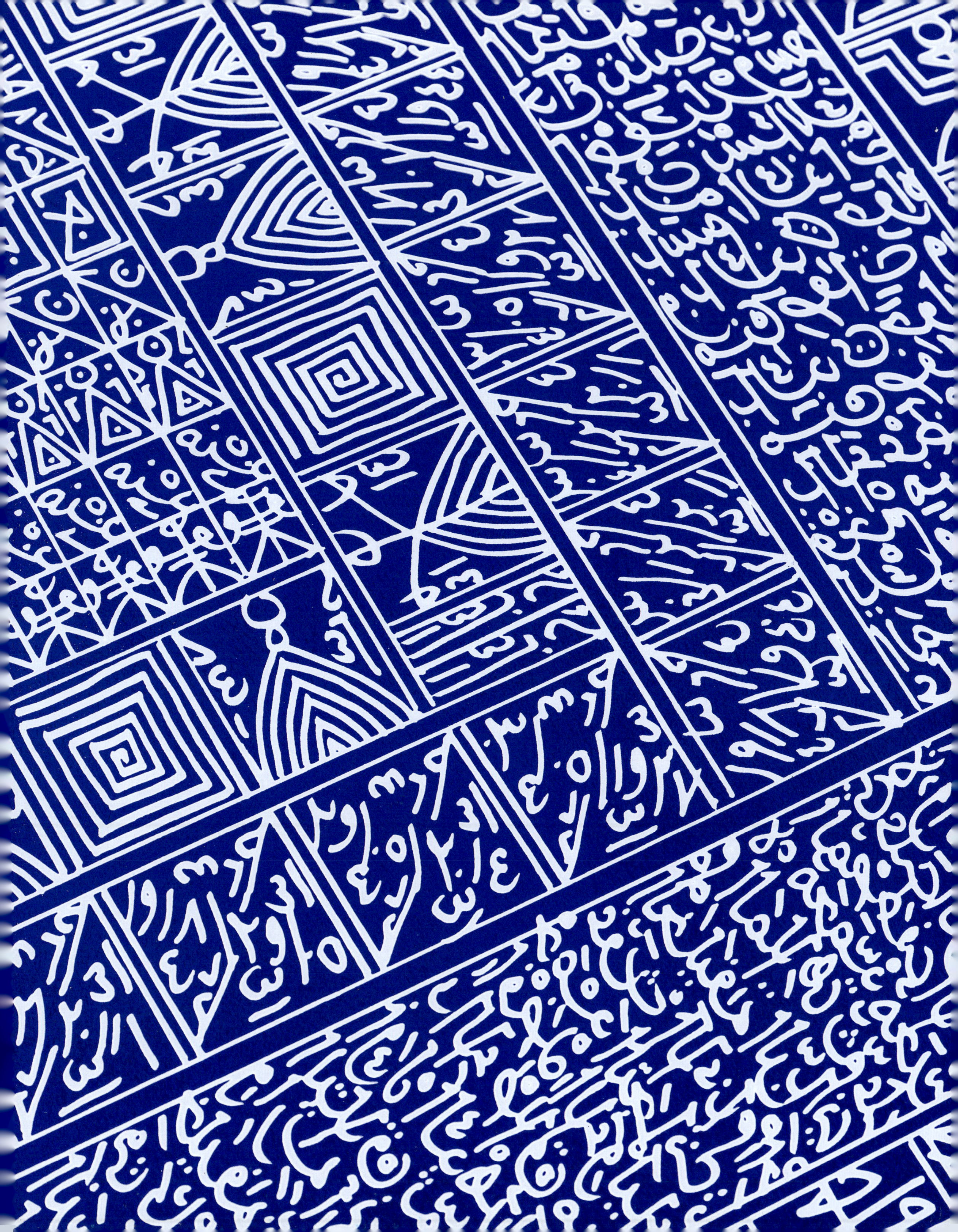

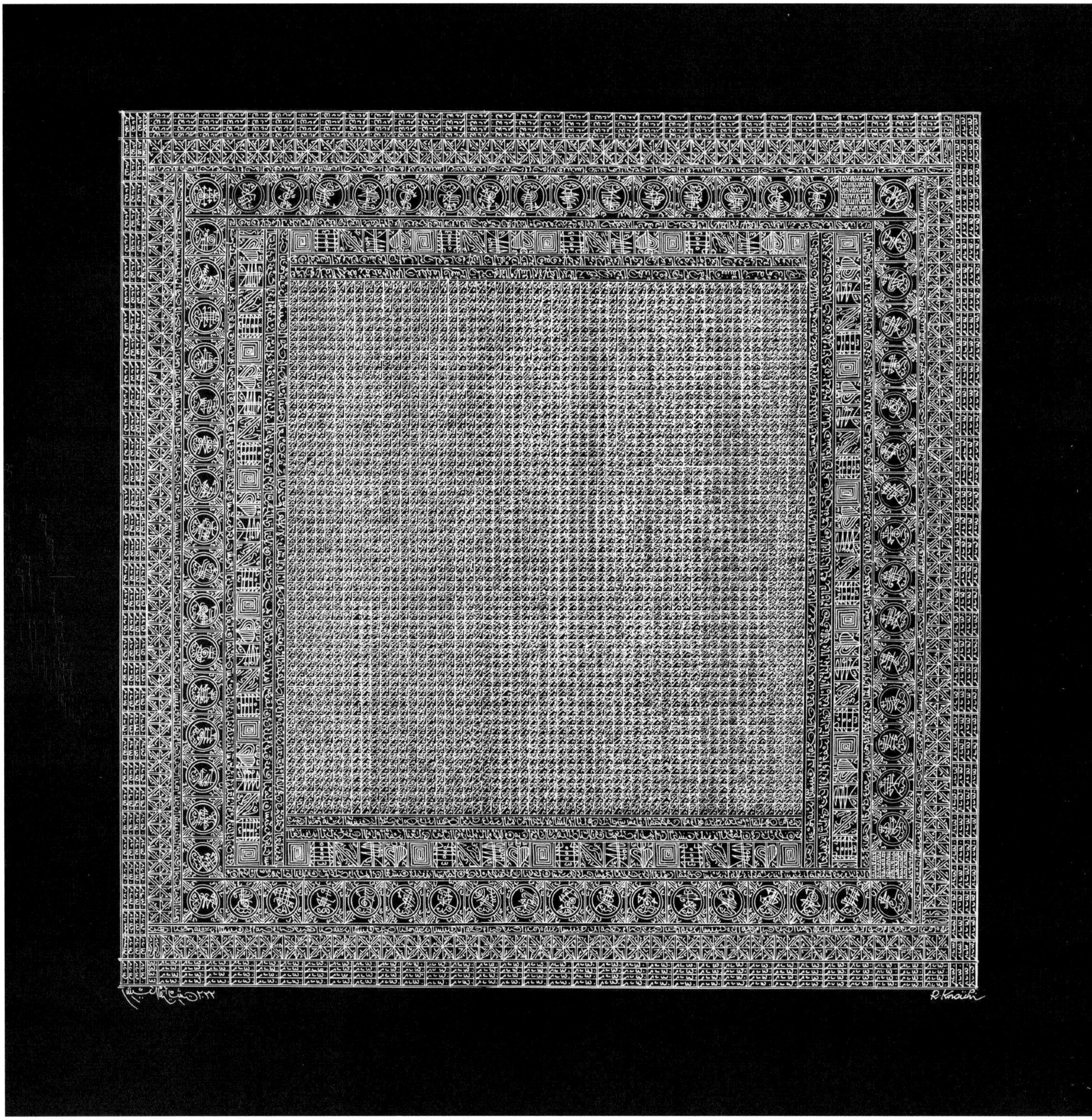

Les ailes bleues des Anges (7) (The Blue of Angels' Wings), 2022.
Acrylic on canvas, 140 x 140 cm.

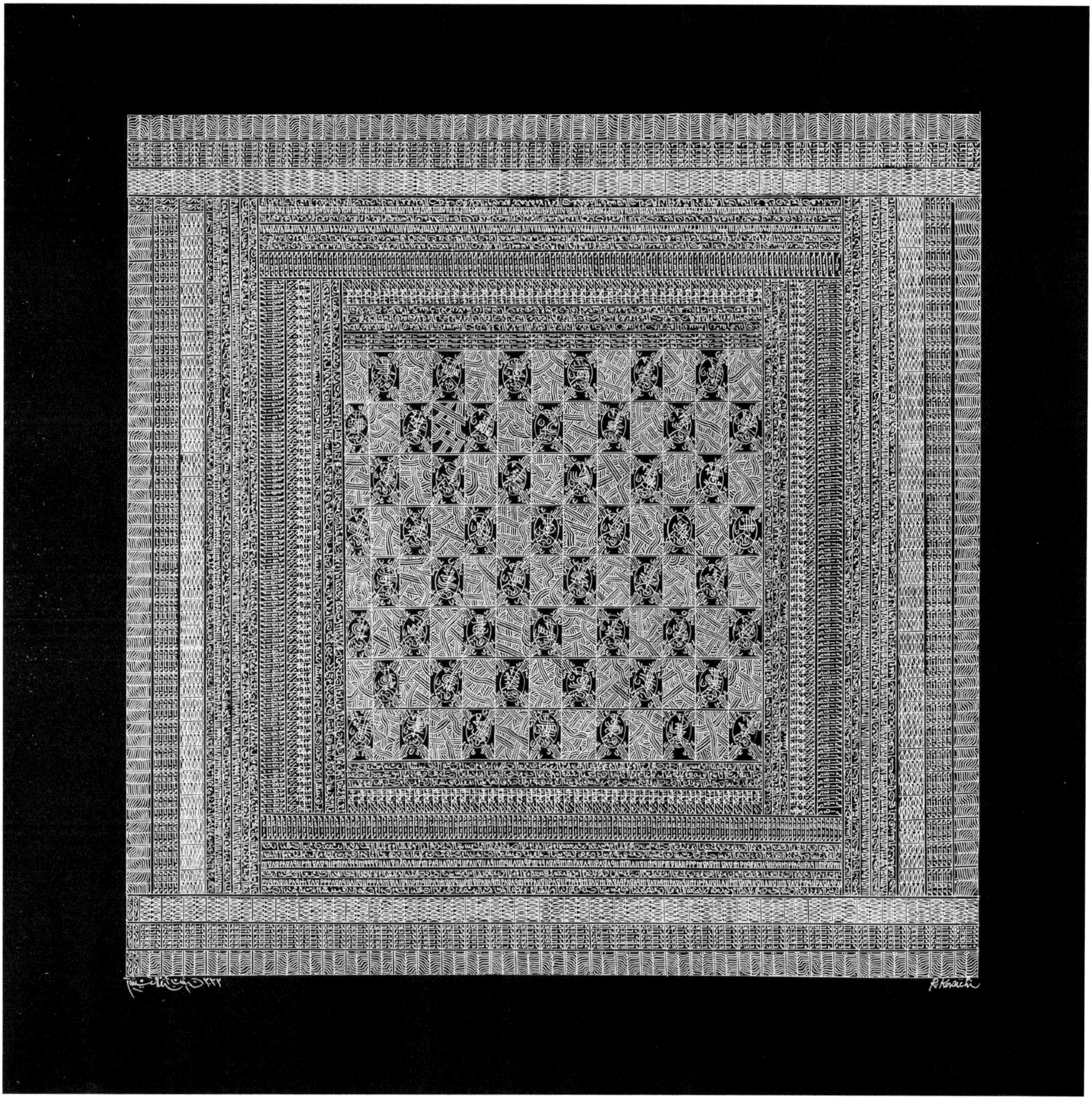

Les ailes bleues des Anges (8) (The Blue of Angels' Wings), 2022.
Acrylic on canvas, 140 x 140 cm.

MIRROR

For humans, writing has become an integral part of our universal heritage. It is an art of life: of imagining our future, recording our present and remembering our past. It makes connections between the hand and the head, between the body and the spirit and between the emotions and purely abstract thought. As I work, I strive to let each line or symbol I inscribe express its own unique internal rhythms. As an example of what that might mean: I can reimagine the Eiffel Tower in ways other than what it might actually represent. To me, for example, it becomes a graphical form; a metallic expression inscribed on the Parisian skies, whose form never ceases to surprise me.

"Would you rather throw stones at a mirror? Come! I am your mirror, here are the stones."
— Rumi

Writing remains a complicated subject. Arabic writing uses individual letters. However, as with the Eiffel Tower analogy, the varying forms of each of those gestural expressions, can suggest all kinds of imagistic overlays. Although many languages exist throughout the Muslim world, prayer itself is only ever performed in Arabic, since this was the language of the Prophet's revelation. Arabic script is therefore understood to be a reflection of the word of God, and it is for this reason that it remains central to our culture.

One reads in the Qur'anic texts the words that God has created us in His likeness, as if we are a mirror image of Him. Since this world is a reflection of that other reality, it is as though everything in the real world exists as a mirror image of that other world. Both Rumi and Ibn 'Arabi repeatedly use the notion of the mirror as a metaphor to explore the qualities and complexities of the interrelationship between the divine Being and the world of creation, and, by extension, between individuals themselves. When I look at myself in the mirror, I see my reflected self in reverse, but believe that is exactly how I am. However, anyone else who looks at me directly sees me the opposite way round to the way I see my reflection in the mirror. Which is the real me?

I frequently use mirror script in my work to underscore this intractable paradox of separation between subject and object, between the world we think we see, which is only a reflection of the real state of being. This reversal of text also operates to provide a kind of equality to spectators who encounter my work. Mirror script writing is difficult to read whether one understands Arabic script or not. So, even for literate Arabic readers, the text becomes opaque and functions at the primary level of graphical forms set down on paper or canvas.

In Rumi's extended masterpiece, *The Quest for the Absolute*, Rumi imagines creation as a mirror in which God contemplates Himself in the act of His own creation. Similarly, Ibn 'Arabi, in his mystical writings and poetry, also uses the traditional metaphor of the heart as a reflective mirror needing to be polished. The more one polishes the mirror of the heart, the better it reflects the ultimate nature of the reality that it seeks to understand.

Right: *Homage to Love and Memory*,
Georgre W. South Memorial Church of the Advocate, Philadelphia, 2007.
A site-specific installation of 21 Banners conceived as a dialogue with and tribute to seven Philadelphia writers, poets and activists.

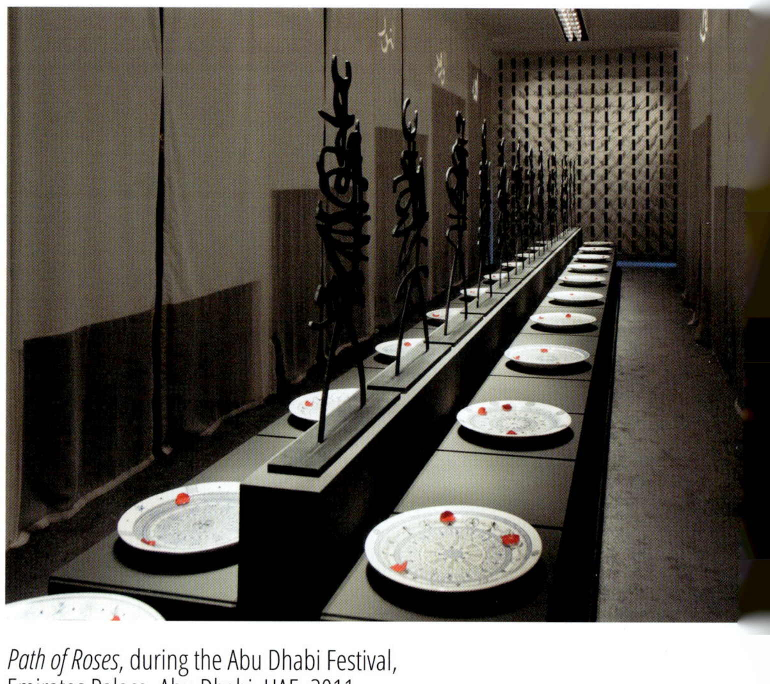

Path of Roses, during the Abu Dhabi Festival,
Emirates Palace, Abu Dhabi, UAE, 2011.

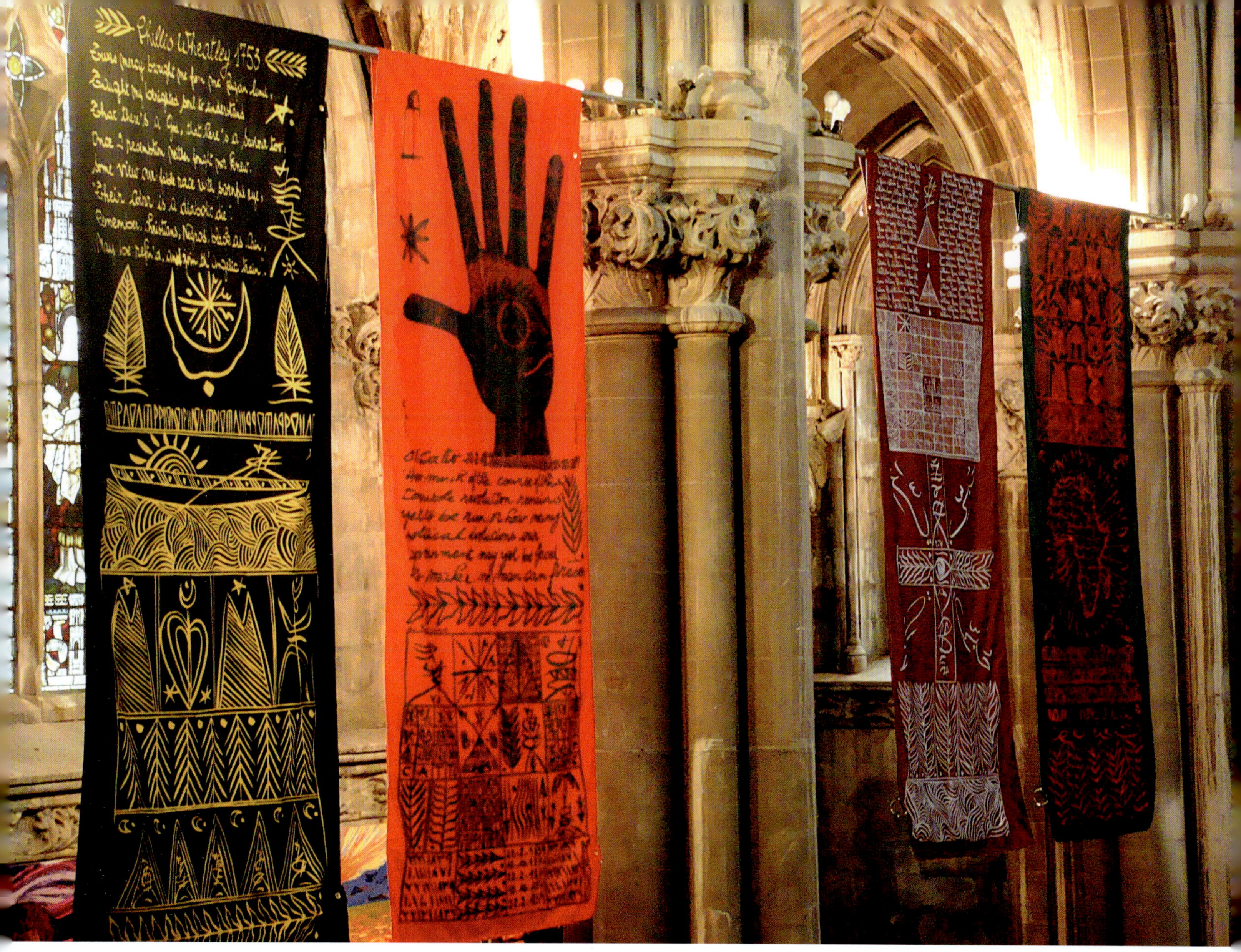

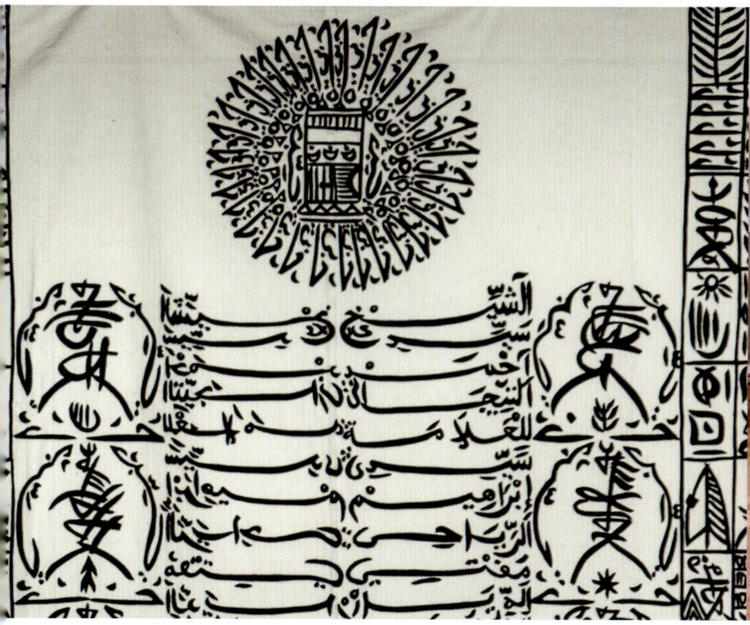

arious examples of mirror script on a banner of *The Invisible Masters.*

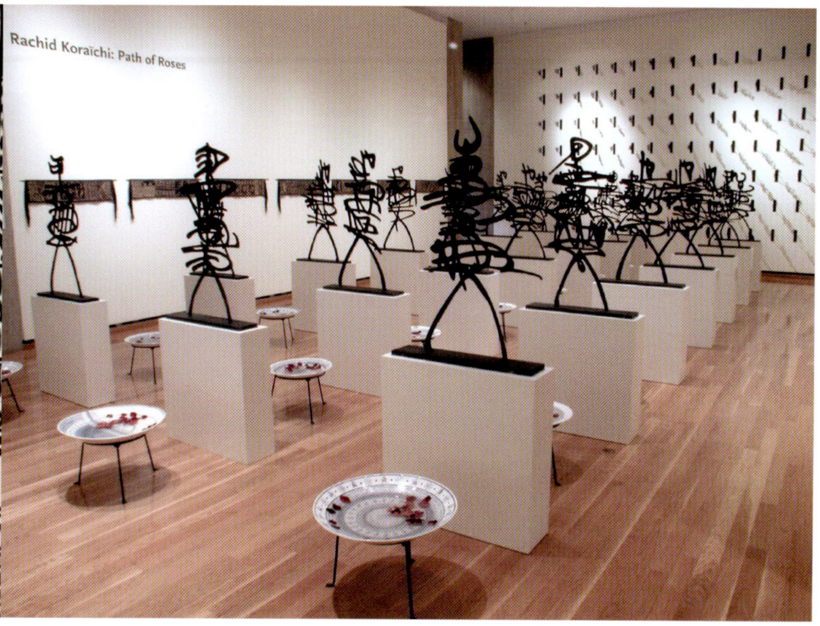

Path of Roses, The Herbert F. Johnson Museum of Art, Cornell University, Ithaca, New York, 2002.

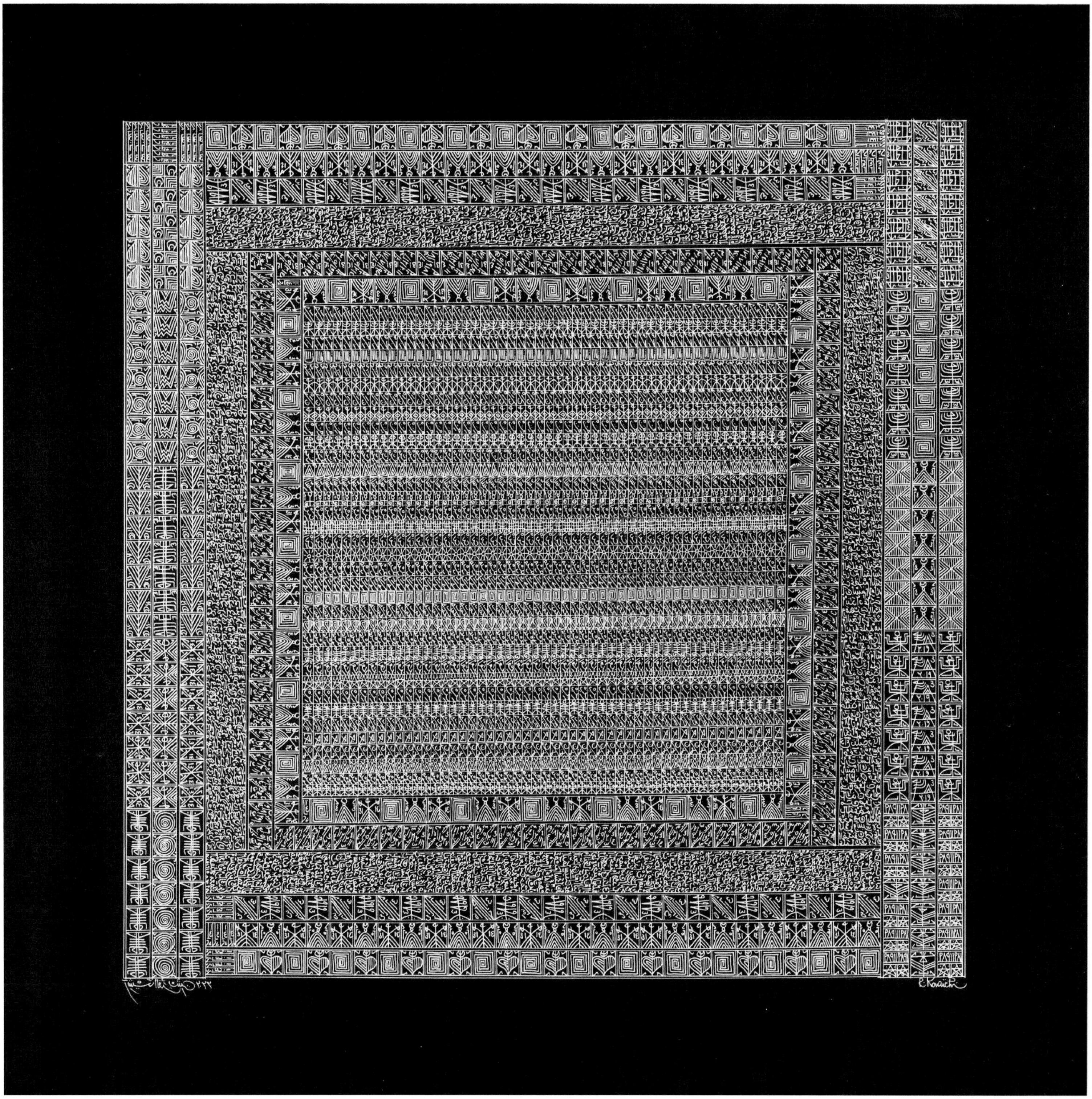

Les ailes bleues des Anges (9) (The Blue of Angels' Wings), 2022.
Acrylic on canvas, 140 x 140 cm.

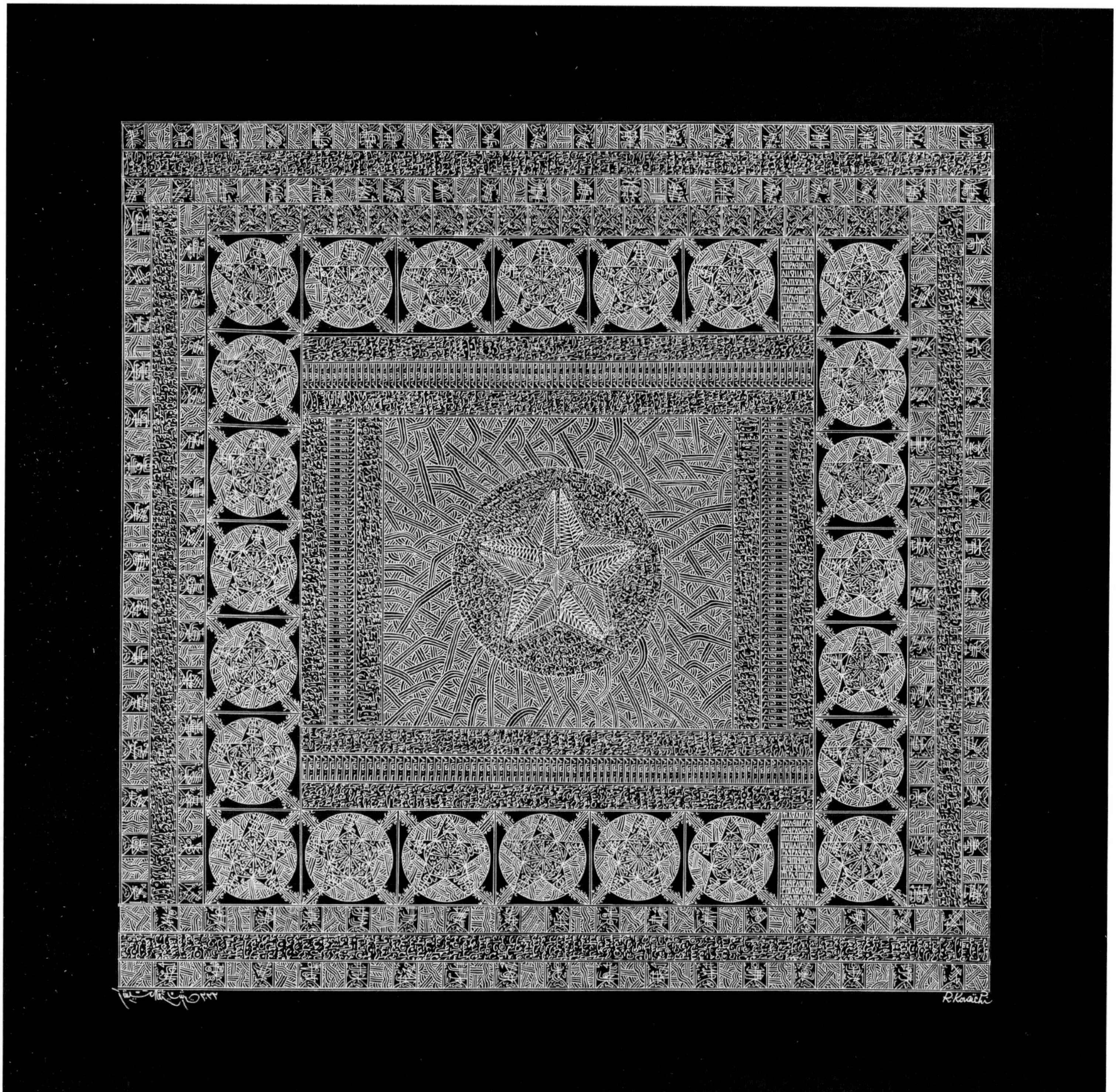

Les ailes bleues des Anges (10) (The Blue of Angels' Wings), 2022.
Acrylic on canvas, 140 x 140 cm.

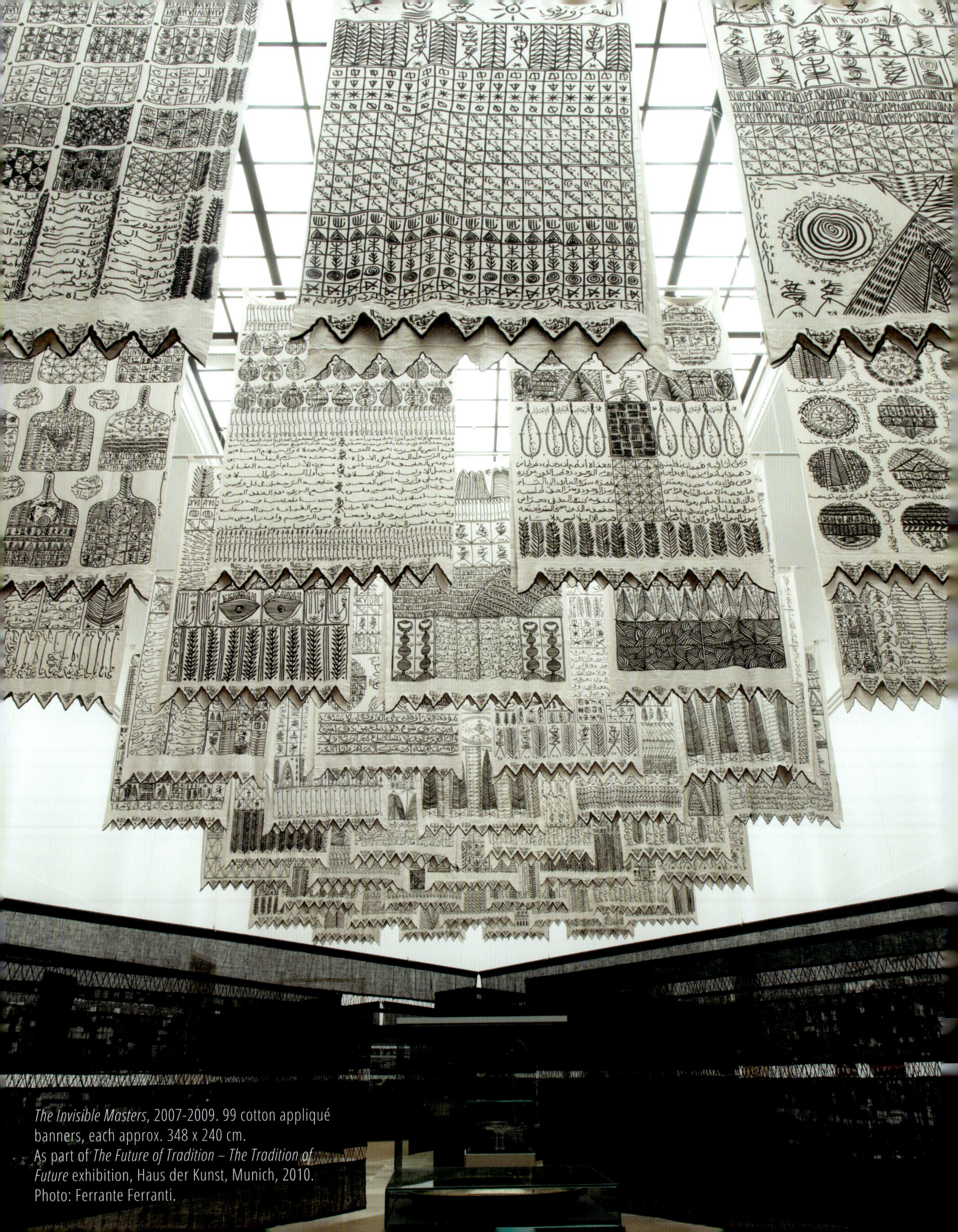

The Invisible Masters, 2007-2009. 99 cotton appliqué banners, each approx. 348 x 240 cm.
As part of *The Future of Tradition – The Tradition of Future* exhibition, Haus der Kunst, Munich, 2010.
Photo: Ferrante Ferranti.

SUFISM AND TOLERANCE

My artistic practice has always drawn on that tradition of Sufi mysticism which is part of my family history and within which I was raised. For many years, I have been working on a grand project that addresses the lives and legacies of the fourteen great mystics of Islam, concerned with the historical development of the broad world of Islam beginning from the western fringes of Andalucia, continuing to the Middle East and on to the further eastern outposts of the Levant. In this broad project, entitled *The Invisible Masters*, I drew together threads in the lives of such great Sufi masters as Jalaluddin al Rumi, Attâr and Ibn 'Arabi, whose fame, both as mystics and poets, has even spread to the west.

"There was a time I would reject those who were not of my faith. But now, my heart has grown capable of taking on all forms."

***— Ibn 'Arabi** (from Interpreter of Desires)*

Less known, but no less important are others, beginning with the extraordinary woman, Rabi'a al-Adawiyya, an 8th century saint who was sold into slavery, and ending with Sheikh Sidi Ahmed al-Tijani and Sheikh Ahmad al-Alawi in the 19th century. My work pays homage to the wisdom of these mystics and strives to highlight the message of universal peace and tolerance transmitted by them all. One could, perhaps, understand this as a chain of initiation whereby each of these past Masters hands the transmission down through the unbroken links of a chain that develops in complex ways over time.

The particular glyph and symbol motifs that ornament my work grew out of the long search I made endeavouring to elaborate a system of signs capable of communicating the universality of these truths. The resulting 'alphabet of memory' – as it has been called – draws not only upon Arabic scripts, but Berber and Tuareg Tifinagh characters, magical squares, talismanic numbers and impromptu ideograms.

For many years now I've been rummaging around in the abundantly furnished wardrobe of the Islamic civilisation to find potentially positive robes in which to dress another image of ourselves and our contemporary civilisation, so as to counter the hackneyed stereotypes by which we are consistently misrepresented in the western media. Muslims are the prime victims of Islamic fundamentalism, and yet, unfortunately, we are constantly tarred with that same brush, and maligned as the root cause of all this excessiveness. To open up to tolerance, as opposed to competitiveness and violence, is of the utmost importance today in order to counter the stereotypical western image of Islam, which all-too-often is confused with islamism. The word Islam, based upon the word *salema* - peace, purity, obedience - translates as 'submission to the will of God,' and implies an absolute obedience to His law.

My overriding intention is to demonstrate that far from the world of Islam being in crisis or being seen as a growing source of unease, tension and violence around the world, there is another perspective entirely. That perspective is clearly set down in the tolerant sophisticated writings of the great Muslim thinkers and poets who have left a large imprint on succeeding generations and who – although no longer bodily present with us today – have left us the unequivocal message that we must build a path towards peaceful and tolerant coexistence. This message is of absolute relevance in light of the ongoing atrocities occurring in Africa, in eastern Europe and in Palestine at this very moment in time.

Below: *7 Indigo Variations* Installation as part of *Textures: Word and Symbol in Contemporary African Art*, Smithsonian, Washington D.C., USA, 2002

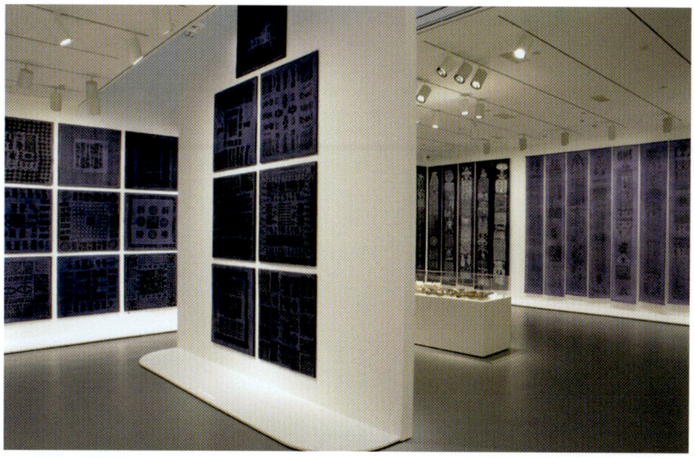

Right: *Les maîtres du temps (Masters of Time)*, October Gallery, London, UK, 2018.

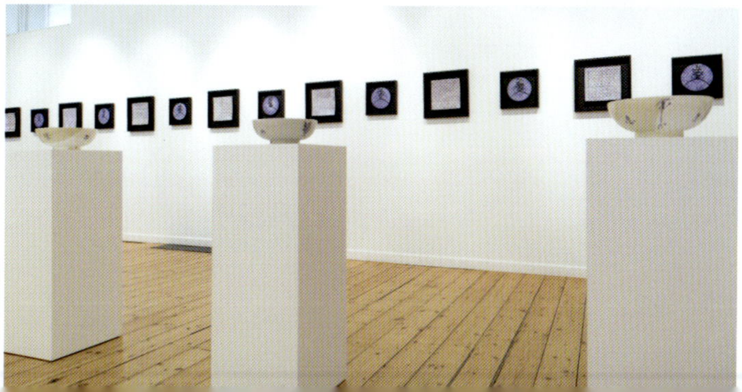

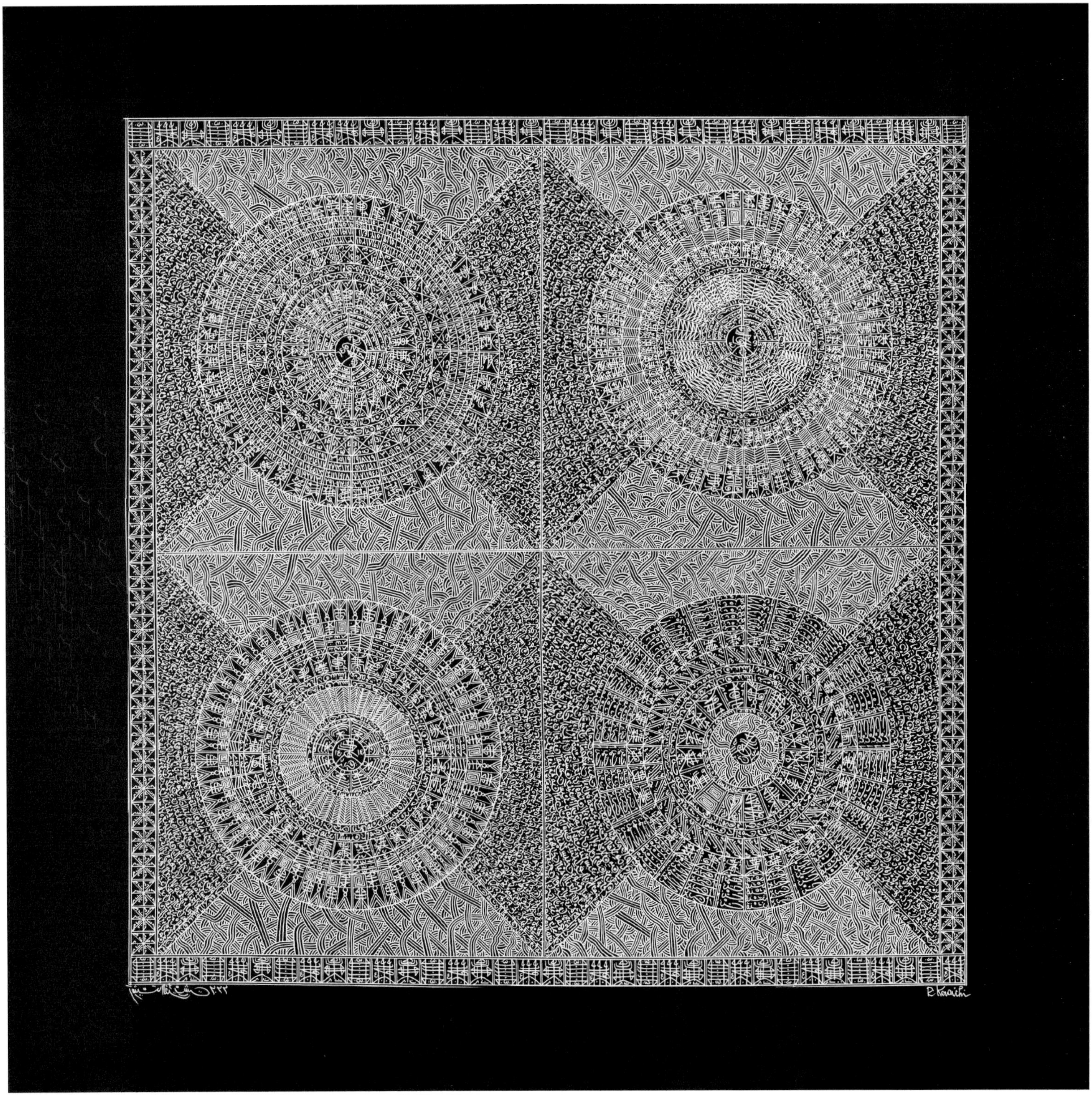

Les ailes bleues des Anges (11) (The Blue of Angels' Wings), 2022.
Acrylic on canvas, 140 x 140 cm.

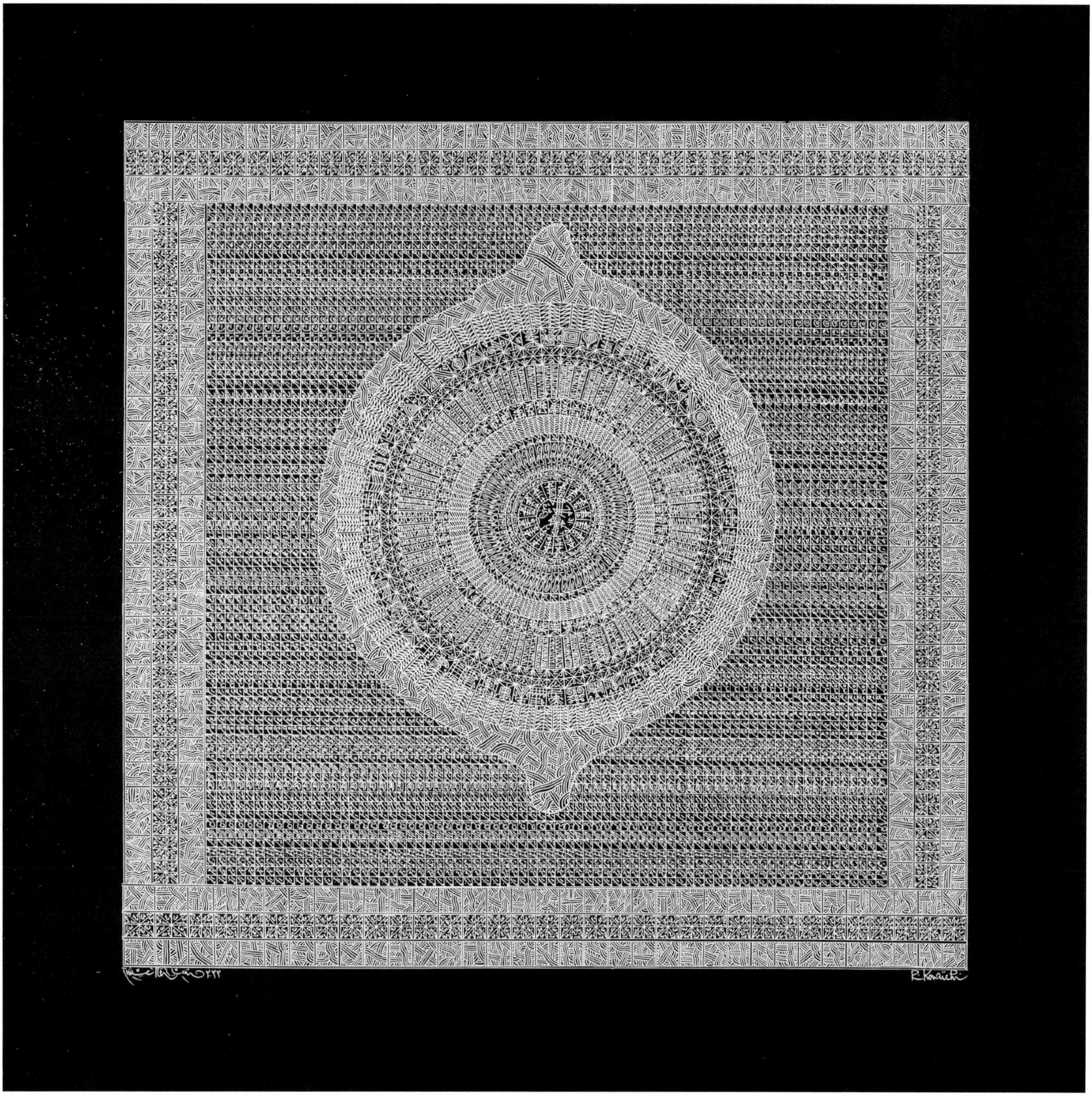

Les ailes bleues des Anges (12) (The Blue of Angels' Wings), 2022.
Acrylic on canvas, 140 x 140 cm.

TOMBS AND MEMORIALS

My work has always supported international Liberation movements, such as the struggles of the peoples of Africa, Vietnam and Palestine, and demonstrated solidarity with immigrants, refugees and all victims of natural and man-made catastrophes. Partly this stems from events experienced during Algeria's War of Independence (1954-1962) and partly from my own fervent beliefs. Following Independence, Algeria descended into a decade-long struggle against islamist militants, resulting in some 250,000 civilian deaths. Such events leave scars on both individual and collective memories, and people become desensitised by repetitive cycles of violence. I am constantly searching for ways to memorialise such difficult occurrences and confront 'man's inhumanity to man.' Because of this, somewhat reluctantly, I have become a designer of memorials.

To work with love…is to charge everything you fashion with the breath of your own spirit, whilst understanding that all the blessed dead are … gathered around, observing what you're doing…

The most recent example, *The Garden of Africa*, arose from my instinctive reaction to the news that the washed-ashore bodies of hundreds of drowned migrants were being unceremoniously thrown onto refuse tips in Zarzis, Tunisia. These corpses, including those of children, are the final remains of refugees, of many nationalities and religions, who die while attempting to cross the Mediterranean Sea in search of a better life.

The violence done to these poor people's remains suggests a world where all humanity has been lost. In response, I decided to create a cemetery, a true Garden of Paradise, for these wretched souls, who remained objects of hatred and rejection even after the horrors of drowning. For me this was very personal, since, when I was 17, my elder brother was pulled out to sea by a rip-tide and drowned. I saw how that accident affected my family, and watched my traumatised mother grieve for her missing son until the day she died. For those who remain behind, the absence of a body to bury leaves only unanswerable questions.

I designed the cemetery as a peaceful sanctuary of contemplation to offer them a dignified final resting place. Each grave carries the results of DNA samples, identificatory elements of the bodies and the date and location of the shipwreck, with the hope of one day helping grieving families find their loved ones again. I wanted these souls to be surrounded by beauty and rest amongst the shade of sweetly-scented trees. This ecumenical cemetery is a memorial to my unknown brothers and sisters and a sincere expression of Fellowship, Tolerance and Humanity. I commissioned Factum Arte to replicate several ancient tombstones of Koraïchi chiefs in Dagestan, and these monumental steles were placed in Zarzis to extend the protection of my Koraïchi ancestors over this private resting ground, which is open and welcoming towards people of all faiths.

Other projects include the memorial I designed at the Château d'Amboise in the Loire. There, the remains of the attendants of the Algerian statesman Emir Abdelkadir (1808–1863), who died of illnesses during his incarceration at the Château, were exhumed from a mass grave and reburied in individual plots. Recognising that these loyal, Muslim followers were unable to perform their sacred duty of pilgrimage to Mecca during their lifetimes, I designed, for each individual, graven headstones whose form recalls the Ka'bah itself. As the sun moves through its daily orbit above the Loire valley, the shadow of the name inscribed within the bronze finials circumambulates each headstone each and every day.

By keeping these silent histories present and alive in our collective memory, they overcome any tendency for these traumatic events to be forgotten, misrepresented or, as becomes increasingly common, even denied outright. As sites of remembrance, these gardens and other memorial monuments become therefore a necessary part of the healing process.

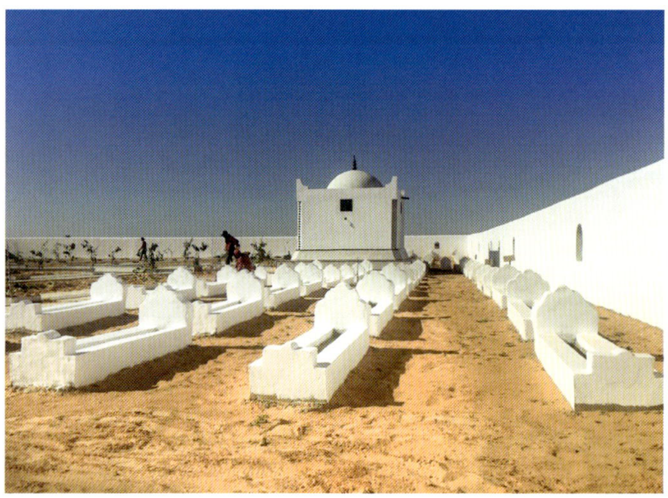

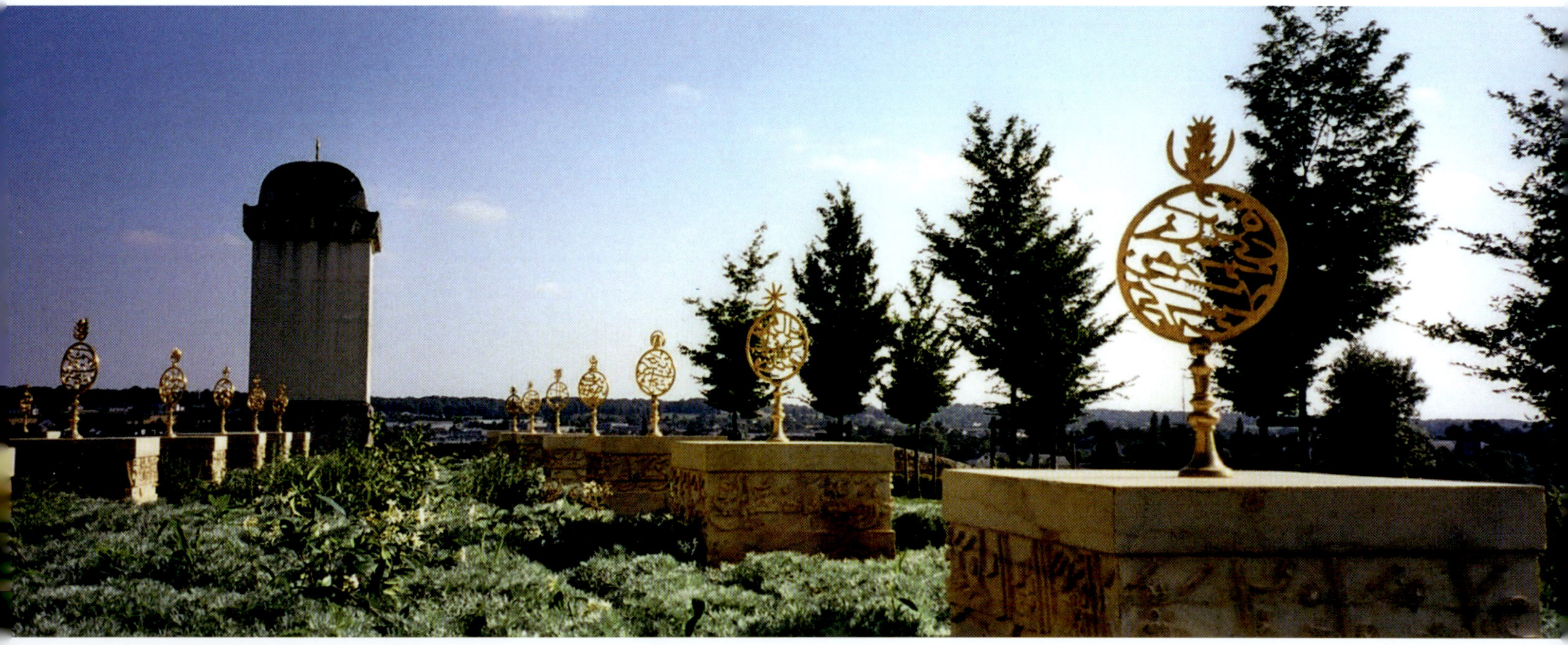

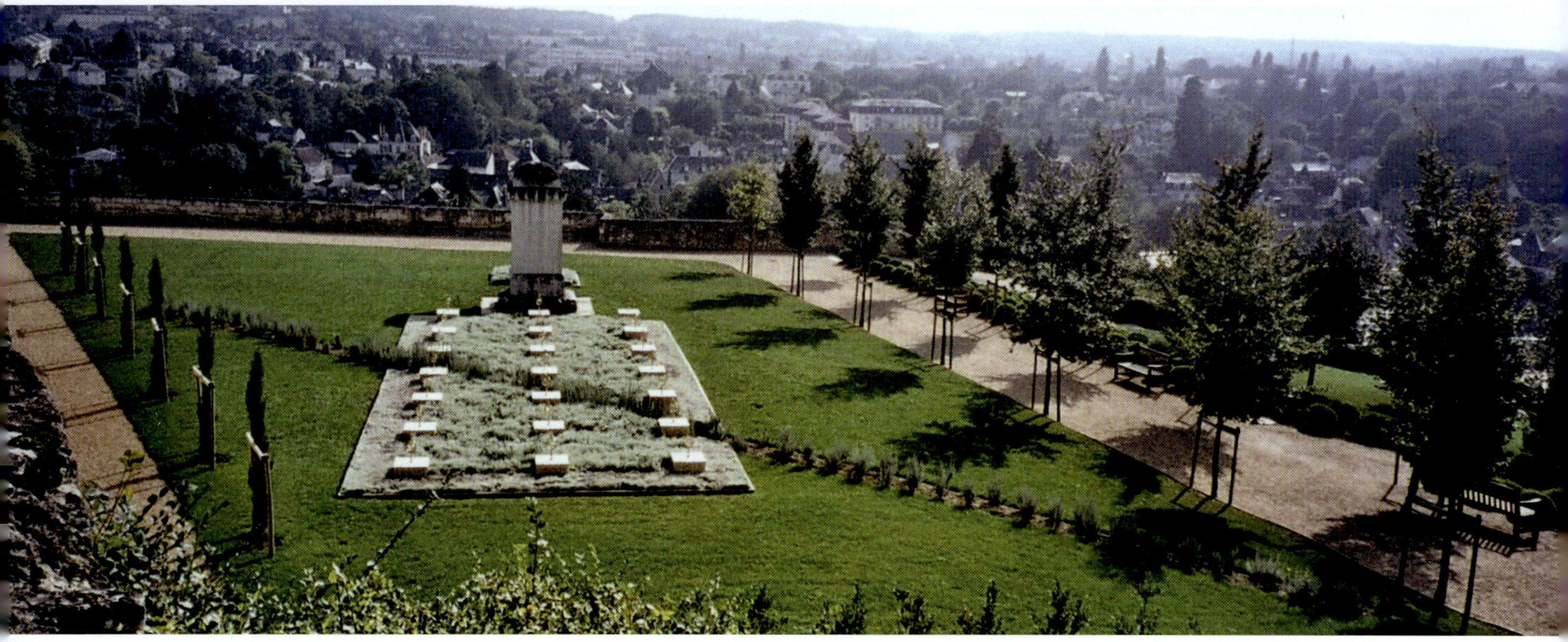

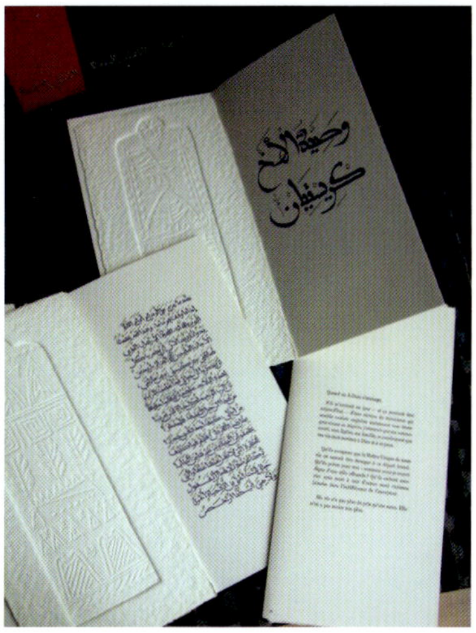

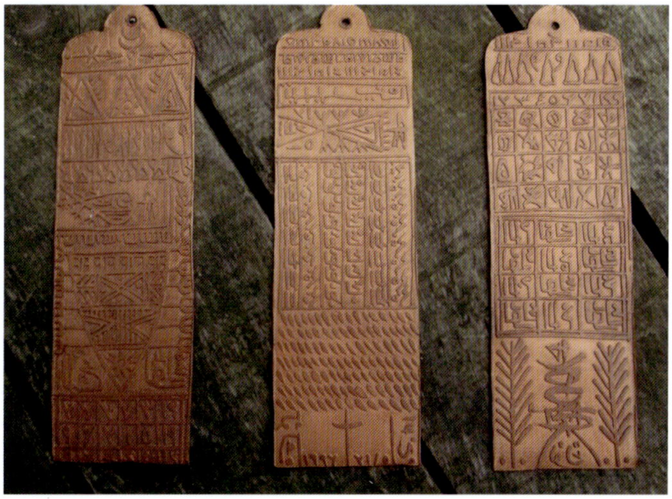

Opposite page:
Graves at the *Garden of Africa* project, Zarzis, Tunisia, early 2021.
Photo courtesy of Rachid Koraïchi.

Above: *Garden of the Orient*, Châteaux d'Amboise, Loire, France, 2005.

Left: Items from *The Seven Sleepers (Les sept dormants)*. Seven Books in Homage to Seven Monks of Tibhirine. Monastery of Tibhirine, Algeria, 2004.

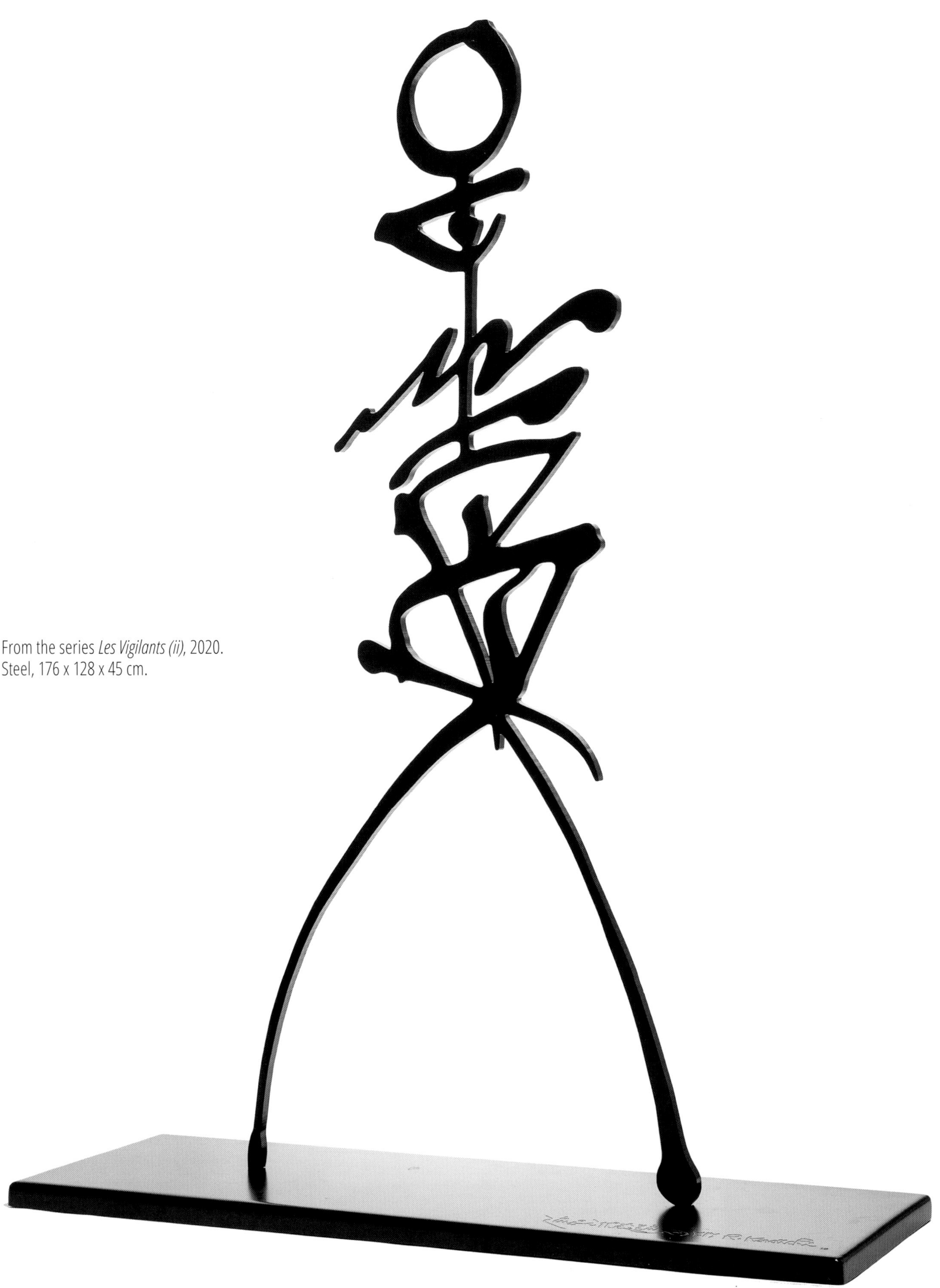

From the series *Les Vigilants (ii)*, 2020.
Steel, 176 x 128 x 45 cm.

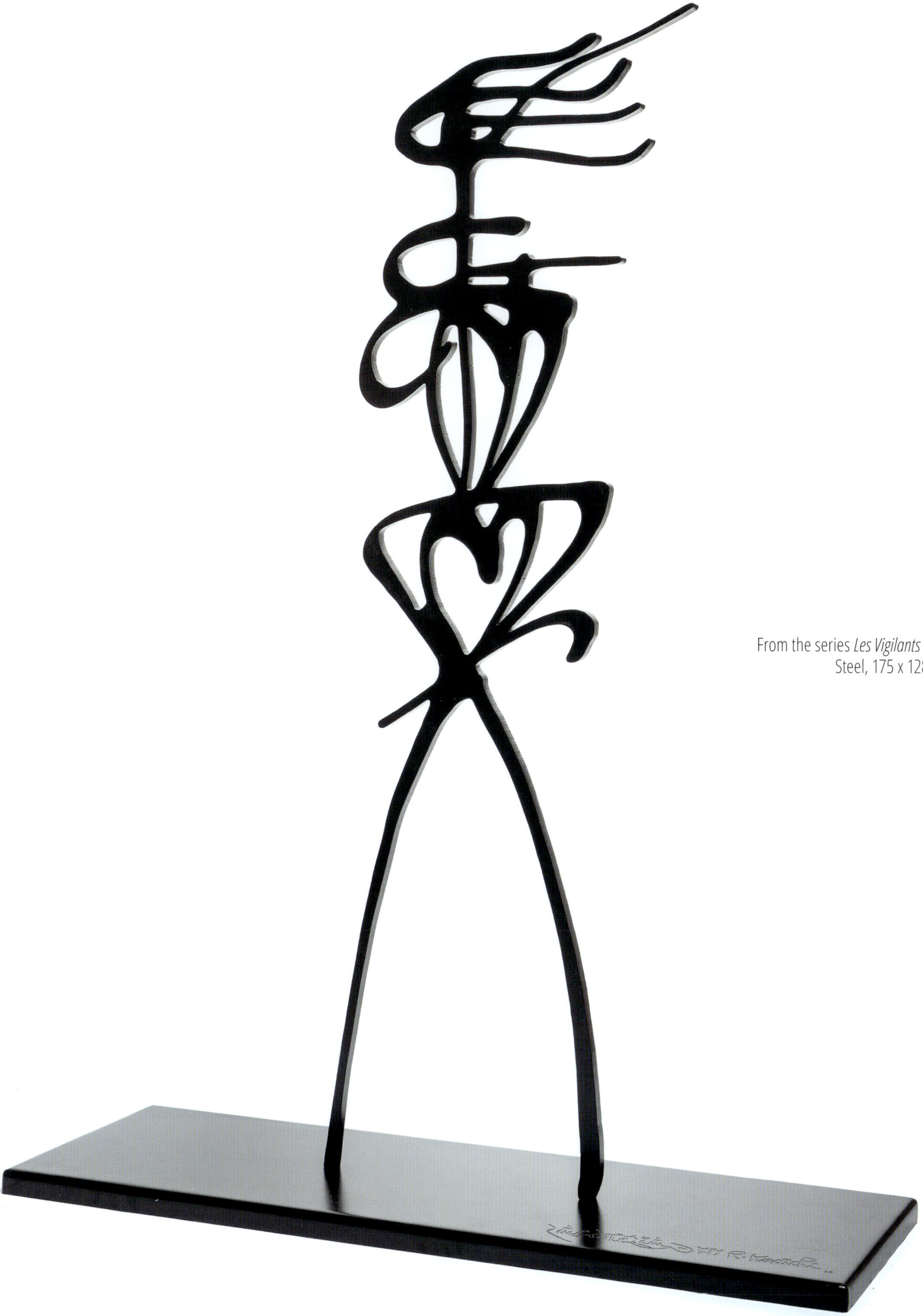

From the series *Les Vigilants (iii)*, 2020.
Steel, 175 x 128 x 45 cm.

RACHID KORAÏCHI

Born in 1947, Aïn Beïda, Algeria. Lives in Paris, France and works across Algeria, Tunisia, Egypt, Europe and beyond.

ART EDUCATION

1967-1971 École supérieure des beaux-arts d'Alger, Algiers, Algeria
1971-1975 École nationale supérieure des arts décoratifs, Paris, France
1973-1975 Institut d'urbanisme, Paris, France
1975-1977 École nationale supérieure des beaux-arts (painting studio of Gustave Singier and print studio of Lagrange-Dorny), Paris, France

SELECTED AWARDS

2013 Prix Institut de France, Fondation Prince Louis de Polignac, Paris, France
2011 Jameel Prize 2011, Victoria and Albert Museum, London, UK

SELECTED PROJECTS

2021 *The Garden of Africa – Jardin d'Afrique*, Zarzis, Tunisia: burial ground and memorial garden for the many migrants drowned while crossing the Mediterranean.

2015 *Dubai Metro Museums Project*, Dubai, UAE: using Koraïchi works of art as external livery on a Dubai metro train.

Ongoing *Dar al Qamar (House of the Moon) and Date Palm Plantation*, El Oued, Algeria. Dar al Qamar: restoration of house in the traditional style as meeting place for local villagers. Date Palm Plantation: sustainable ecological system exploring ancient horticultural and conservation techniques.

Ongoing *Mausoleum of the Ancestors*, Kouinine, Algeria: restoration and conservation of an important historical monument.

2013 *Waste Water Gardens*, Témacine, Algeria: restoration of a ruined but historically significant Ksar (fortified village) and (in association with the Institute of Ecotechnics) implementation of a sustainable ecological garden as raw sewage treatment system.

2009 *Association Schams*, Témacine, Algeria: foundation established to provide skills and nurture hope among unemployed local youths by engaging them in community based craft projects.

2005 *Jardin d'Orient – The Garden of the Orient*, Château Royal d'Amboise, Amboise, France: garden of repose to memorialise those followers of Emir Abdelkader, who were formerly buried there in a mass grave.

1995 *Dar Koraïchi*, Medina of Tunis, Tunisia: complete restoration of this historic house (Dar General Ben Turkia) in the traditional style, working in collaboration with local craftsmen.

SELECTED SOLO EXHIBITIONS

2024 *Celestial Blue*, October Gallery, London, UK
Rachid Koraïchi: An Ode to Intertwined Histories, Elmarsa Gallery, Dubai, UAE

2023 *My Shadow Misses You*, Khawla Art & Culture Foundation, Khawla Art Gallery, Dubai, UAE

2022 *Le Chant de l'Ardent Désir*, Aicon Gallery, New York, USA

2021 *Tears that Taste of the Sea*, October Gallery, London, UK

2019 *This Long Journey into Your Gaze (Este largo viaje hasta tu mirada)*, Casa Árabe, Madrid; Casa Árabe, Córdoba, Spain (in collaboration with Factum Arte, Madrid)
Frieze New York, USA (with Aicon Gallery, New York, USA)

2018 *Les Maîtres du Temps (Masters of Time)*, October Gallery, London, UK
Les Sept Stations Célestes | The Seven Heavenly Stations, Aicon Gallery, New York, USA

2017 *Les Ancêtres liés aux Étoiles*, A2Z Art Gallery, Paris, France

2016 *Love Side by Side with the Soul*, Aicon Gallery, New York, USA
ArtBahrain, Manama, Bahrain (with A2Z Art Gallery, Paris, France)

2015 *Il n'est d'autres souverains que ceux qui me regardent*, Elmarsa Gallery, Dubai, UAE

2011 *Une Nation en Exil (A Nation in Exile)*, Montauban, France
Path of Roses (Tariq al-Ward), Abu Dhabi Festival, Emirates Palace, in association with ADMAF (Abu Dhabi Music & Arts Foundation), Abu Dhabi, UAE

2010 *Rachid Koraïchi: Ecstatic Flow*, October Gallery, London, UK

2008 *Les Ancêtres liés aux Étoiles (Ancestors Linked to the Stars)*, Chapelle Saint Martin, Le Méjan, Arles, France
Chemin des Roses (Path of Roses), Citadel of Algiers, Algiers, Algeria
Hommage à Mahmoud Darwich, Institut du Monde Arabe, Paris, France

2007 *20 Years: 12 Poets: Ceramics by Rachid Koraïchi*, Institute for the Humanities, University of Michigan, Ann Arbor, Michigan, USA
A Nation in Exile (Une Nation en Exil), Galerie 23, Amsterdam, the Netherlands
Homage to Love and Memory, The George W. South Memorial, Church of the Advocate, Philadelphia, USA

2005 *Ancestral Memories*, October Gallery, London, UK

2004 *Alep, Voyage en Soi(e) of Rachid Koraïchi*, Galerie Isma, Riadh el Feth, Algiers, Algeria
Rachid Koraïchi: 7 Variations Indigo, Musée de la Vieille Charité, Marseille, France

2002 *Path of Roses (Chemin des Roses) / Beirut's Poem (Poème de Beyrouth) / A Nation in Exile (Une Nation en Exil)*, The Herbert F. Johnson Museum of Art, Cornell University, Ithaca, New York, USA
Une Nation en Exil, United Nations, Beirut, Lebanon

2001 *Beirut's Poem (Poème de Beyrouth) and Path of Roses (Chemin des Roses)*, Jordan National Gallery of Fine Art, Amman, Jordan; Institut Français, Casablanca; Institut Français, Marrakech, Morocco
Hommage à Ibn 'Arabi, Church of Mérignac, Mérignac, France; The Khalid Shoman Foundation - Darat al Funun, Amman, Jordan

2000 *Rencontre à Casablanca (Meeting in Casablanca)*, joint exhibition with Farid Belkahia, Gallery Al Manar, Casablanca, Morocco
Anthologie de poésie arabe (Anthology of Arab Poems), National Library, Limoges, France
Interfaces, The Bachelard Amphitheatre of the Sorbonne, Paris, France

1999 *Chemin des Roses I, hommage à Rûmî (Path of Roses I, Homage to Rûmî)*, Residency at the Institut Français, Anatolia, Turkey
Autour des voyages de Delacroix et Matisse (Around the Travels of Delacroix and Matisse), Residency in Marrakech, Morocco
Ô Fleurs! Hommage à Attar (Oh Flowers! Homage to Attar), International Garden Festival, Chaumont-sur-Loire, France

1998 *Lettres d'Argile : Hommage à Ibn 'Arabi (Letters of Clay: Homage to Ibn 'Arabi* (touring 1998-1999), Espace Gard, Nîmes, France, touring to Institut Français and Darat al-Funun, Amman, Jordan; Institut Français, Damascus, Syria; Al-Mustansiriya Madrasah, Baghdad, Iraq; Institut Français, Ribat de Sousse, Tunisia; National Francophone Multimedia Library of Limoges, France; Gallery Isma, Algiers, Algeria; Museum of Contemporary Art, Caracas, Venezuela; Embassy of France, Algiers, Algeria; Gallery A. Gorgi, Sidi Bou Saïd, Tunisia; Institut Français, Tunis, Tunisia
Rachid Koraïchi: Clay, Silk, Paper & Steel, Leighton House Museum, London, UK
Le Jardin du Paradis (The Garden of Paradise), International Garden Festival, Chaumont-sur-Loire, France
Anthologie de poésie arabe (Anthology of Arab Poems), Elsa Triolet and Jules Verne Library, Pantin, France
Soie et Argile (Silk and Clay), The Khalid Shoman Foundation, Darat al-Funun, Amman, Jordan, in cooperation with AFAA and the Institut Français, Amman, Jordan

1997 *L'Enfant-Jazz* (touring 1997-2000), Institut du Monde Arabe, Paris, France; Studio Franck Bordas, Paris, France; County Centre for Educational Documentation, Avignon, France; Collège des Hautes Vallées, Guillestre, France; Sakakini Foundation, Ramallah, Palestine; Passage de l'art, Marseille, France
Hommage à Okba (Homage to Okba), Steel Sculpture, University of Kairouan, Tunisia
Hommage à René Char, Michel Butor, Mohammed Dib (Homage to René Char, Michel Butor, Mohammed Dib), Monumental Tapestry, National Francophone Multimedia Library of Limoges, France
A Nation in Exile (Une Nation en Exil), The Khalid Shoman Foundation, Darat al-Funun, Amman, Jordan

1996 *Ceramic Wall*, with students of the Robert Desnos School, Tunis, Tunisia

1995 *Objects and Decor for La Reine Didon (Queen Dido)*, Antique Theatre of Carthage, Festival of Carthage, Tunisia
Installation, Haus der Kulturen der Welt, Berlin, Germany
Talisman (Fountain Mural), Palm Beach, Tozeur, Tunisia
Hymnes Gravés (Engraved Hymns), Institut Français, Barcelona, Spain

1994 Exhibition at Gallery Schauer, Paris, France
Exhibition at Gallery Yahya, Tunis, Tunisia

1993 *Nuits d'Encens (Nights of Incense)*, Homage to Algiers, Antique Theatre of Carthage, Tunisia
Les Sept Portes du Ciel (The Seven Gates of Heaven), Artibule, Institut Français, Casablanca, Morocco; Tour de Constance, Aigues-Mortes, France
Carpets and Tapestries, Gallery A. Gorgi, Sidi Bou Saïd, Tunisia

1992 Exhibition at Galerie Cherif Fine Art, Sidi Bou Saïd, Tunisia
Exhibition at Gallery Ipso, Brussels, Belgium
Salomé, Tobacco Factory, Ajaccio, Corsica; Artibule, Institut Français, Casablanca, Morocco
Exhibition at Galerie Jaqueline Moussion, Paris, France
Exhibition at Modern Art Museum, Liège, Belgium

1991 *L'Art contemporain (Contemporary Art)*, Institut du Monde Arabe, Paris, France
Exhibition at Gallery Editart, Geneva, Switzerland
Havana Biennial, Wilfredo Lam Centre, Havana, Cuba
Exhibition at Gallery Ipso, Brussels, Belgium

1990 *Salomé (joint exhibition with Michel Butor)*, Centre Georges Pompidou, Paris, France; Institut du Monde Arabe, Paris, France

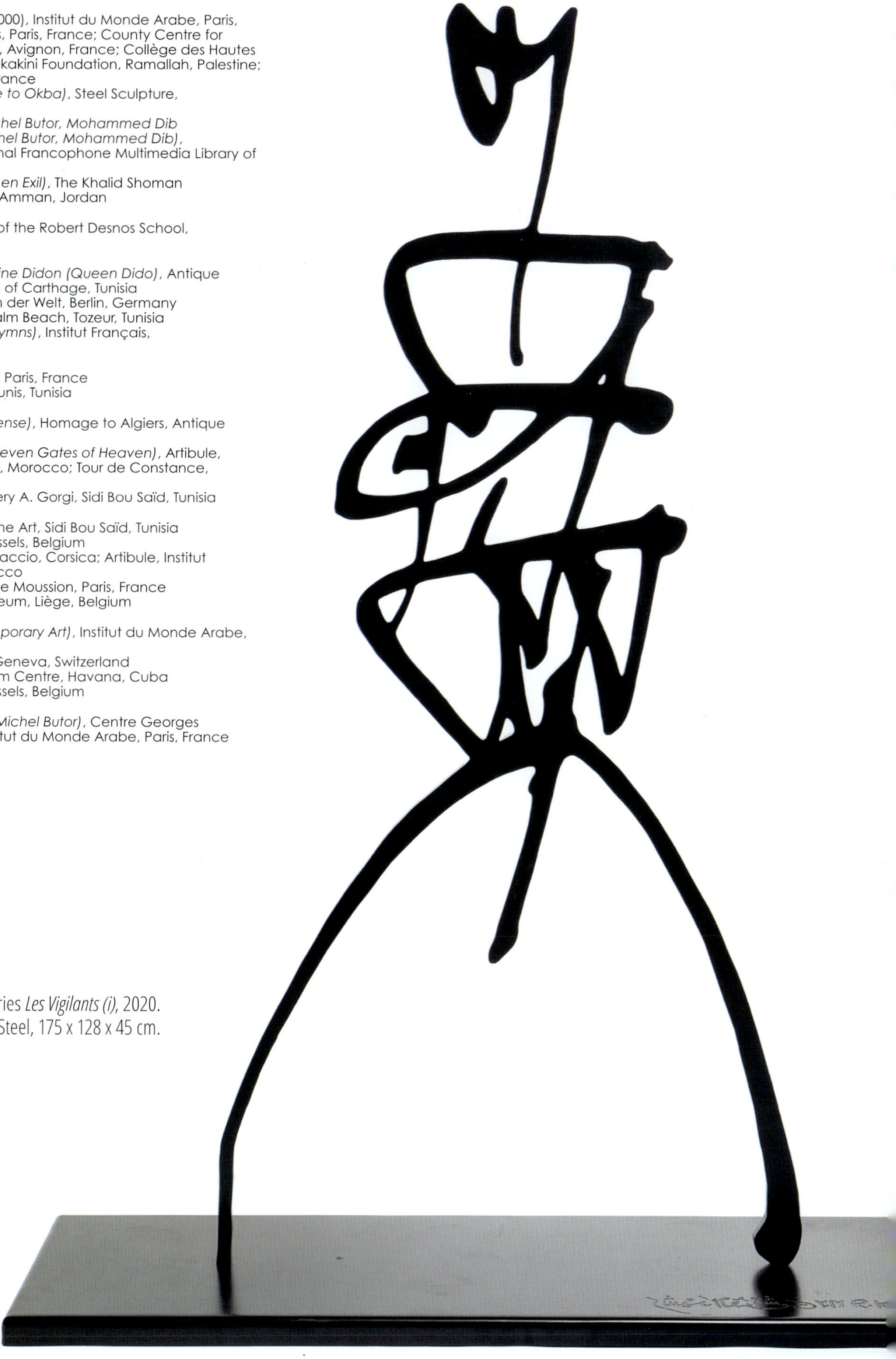

From the series *Les Vigilants (i)*, 2020.
Steel, 175 x 128 x 45 cm.

SELECTED GROUP EXHIBITIONS

2023 *Unhealed*, Moderna Museet, Malmö, Sweden

2022 *Nomadic Resonance*, October Gallery, London, UK

2021-22 *Writing is drawing*, Centre Pompidou-Metz, Metz, France

2021 *Contemporary Ceramic Art from the Middle East*, Victoria and Albert Museum, London, UK

2020 *Atmospheres: Artists of the Transvangarde*, October Gallery, London, UK
Between the Sun and the Moon, Lahore Biennale 02, Lahore Museum, Lahore, Pakistan

2019 *Dream No Small Dream: Celebrating 40 Years of the Transvangarde*, October Gallery, London, UK
Abu Dhabi Art Fair, Abu Dhabi, UAE (with October Gallery, London, UK)
Dix ans déjà !, A2Z Art Gallery, Paris, France

2018 *Al Musiqa*, Cité de la musique - Philharmonie de Paris, Paris, France
Sahara: What is Written Will Remain, Gallerie delle Prigioni, Treviso, Italy
Calligraphy as Process from East Asia, the Middle East, North Africa, Europe and the Americas, Garage Cosmos, Brussels, Belgium
Installation of sculptures from the series *Les Prieurs* and of acid etched steel plates *Hommage a Tierno Bokar, African Talisman* at Masterpiece Art Fair, London, UK (with Factum Arte, Madrid)

2017 *Interwoven Dialogues: Contemporary Art from Africa and South Asia*, Aicon Gallery, New York, USA
Tour du monde en tondo, Musée de l'Hospice Saint-Roch, Issoudun, France (in collaboration with Galerie Claude Lemand, Paris, France)
As Above, So Below: Portals, Visions, Spirits & Mystics, IMMA (Irish Museum of Modern Art), Dublin, Ireland
100 chefs-d'œuvre de l'art moderne et contemporain arabe, Institut du Monde Arabe, Paris, France
Trésor de l'Islam en Afrique, Institut du Monde Arabe, Paris, France

2016 *Not New Now*, Marrakech Biennale, Marrakech, Morocco
Installation of 49 banners of *The Invisible Masters* at Carreau du Temple, AKAA, Paris, France (with October Gallery, London, UK)
Jardins d'Orient de l'Alhambra au Taj Mahal, Institut du Monde Arabe, Paris, France
Wondrous Worlds: Art & Islam Through Time & Place, Newark Museum, Newark, New Jersey, USA
Rencontre, émotions partagées, A2Z Art Gallery, Paris, France

2015 *Positif Exil*, 19 Paul Fort, Paris, France
Nel Mezzo del Mezzo, Museo RISO, Regional Museum of Modern and Contemporary Art, Palermo, Italy
International Arabic Calligraphy Exhibition, Wafi Mall, Dubai, UAE
Expanding Africa at the Newark Museum: New Visions, New Galleries, Newark Museum, Newark, New Jersey, USA

2014 *Seeing Through Light: Selections from the Guggenheim Abu Dhabi Collection*, Guggenheim Abu Dhabi, Abu Dhabi, UAE
The Global Africa Project: Political Patterns, Seoul Museum of Art, Seoul, South Korea
Biennale Internationale de Casablanca, Casablanca, Morocco
ArteVida, Museum of Modern Art, Rio de Janeiro, Brazil
35 Years of the Transvangarde: Contemporary art from around the Planet, October Gallery, London, UK

2013 *Qalam, the Art of Beautiful Writing*, Birmingham Museums & Art Gallery, UK
Symbiosis of Two Worlds, Palais Namaskar, Marrakech, Morocco (in collaboration with Written Art Foundation, Frankfurt, Germany)
Masters of the Transvangarde, October Gallery, London, UK
Trade Routes, Hauser & Wirth, London, UK

2012 *Dieu(x): Modes d'Emploi*, Petit Palais (Musée des Beaux Arts de la Ville de Paris), Paris, France
Reflections from Heaven, Meditations on Earth: Modern Calligraphic Art from the Arab World, (touring 2012-2013) Museum of the Imperial Forums, Rome, Italy; and Museo Valencia de la Illustración y la Modernidad Valencia, Spain (organised by the Jordan National Gallery of Fine Arts & The Museum of the Imperial Forums, Rome, Italy)

2011 *Jameel Prize 2011*, (touring 2011- 2013) Victoria and Albert Museum, London, UK; Institut du Monde Arabe, Paris, France; Casa Árabe, Madrid, Spain; Cantor Arts Center, Stanford University, San Francisco, USA; and San Antonio Museum of Art, San Antonio, Texas, USA
Written Images: Contemporary Calligraphy from the Middle East, (touring 2011-2012) Sundaram Tagore Gallery, New York, USA; and Sundaram Tagore Gallery, Hong Kong

2010 *The Future of Tradition – The Tradition of Future*, Haus der Kunst, Munich, Germany (first complete installation of *The Invisible Masters / Les Maîtres Invisibles*)
The Global Africa Project, Museum of Arts and Design, New York, USA
Miragens, (touring 2010-2011) Centro Cultural Banco do Brasil (CCBB), São Paulo; Rio de Janeiro; Brasilia, Brazil

2009 *The Essential Art of African Textiles: Design Without End*, Metropolitan Museum of Art, New York, USA

2008 *The Poetics of Cloth*, Grey Art Gallery NYU, New York, USA
Les Ancêtres liés aux Étoiles (Ancestors Linked to the Stars), Chapelle Saint Martin, Le Méjan, Arles, France
Word into Art (a British Museum touring exhibition), The Atrium, DIFC, Dubai, UAE
Angaza Afrika: African Art Now, October Gallery, London, UK

2007 *The Dance of Quill and Ink, Contemporary Art of the Middle East*, State Hermitage Museum, St. Petersburg, Russia (in association with the Triumph Gallery, Moscow, Russia)
Inscribing Meaning: Writing and Graphic Systems in African Art, National Museum of African Art, Smithsonian Institution, Washington D.C., USA

2006 *Without Boundary: Seventeen Different Ways of Looking*, MoMA, New York, USA
Text Messages, October Gallery, London, UK
Word into Art, British Museum, London, UK

2005 *The Seven Gates of Heaven (Les Sept Portes du Ciel)* and an aliquot sample from *Path of Roses (Chemin des Roses)*, British Museum, London, UK
TEXTures: Word and Symbol in Contemporary African Art, National Museum of African Art, Smithsonian Institution, Washington D.C., USA

2004 *Intelligence Now!*, October Gallery, London, UK

2003 *Voyages d'Artistes, Algérie 2003*, Espace EDF – Electra, Paris, France
Africa Informs, October Gallery, London, UK
Répliques, (light installations curated by Philippe Mouillon), Tunnel des Facultés, Algiers, Algeria
Fragments of Script, Comédie Française, Paris, France

2002 *A la nuit tombée (At Nightfall)*, (light installations curated by Philippe Mouillon), Quais de l'Isère, Grenoble, France

2001 *Unpacking Europe*, Museum Boijmans Van Beuningen, Rotterdam, the Netherlands
Authentic/Ex-centric, 49th Venice Biennale, Venice, Italy
The Short Century - Independence and Liberation Movements in Africa 1945-1994, (touring 2001-2002) Museum Villa Stuck, Munich, Germany; Martin-Gropius-Bau, Berlin, Germany; Museum of Contemporary Art, Chicago, USA; PS1 Contemporary Art Centre; and the Museum of Modern Art, New York, USA